# ONTOLOGIES AND DATABASES



*edited by*

**Athman Bouguettaya**
*Queensland University of Technology*

*A Special Issue of*
**DISTRIBUTED AND PARALLEL DATABASES**
**An International Journal**
**Volume 7, No. 1 (1999)**

**KLUWER ACADEMIC PUBLISHERS**
**Boston / Dordrecht / London**

# DISTRIBUTED AND PARALLEL DATABASES

Volume 7, No. 1, January 1999

**Special Issue: Ontologies and Databases**
**Guest Editor: Athman Bouguettaya**

**Distributors for North, Central and South America:**
Kluwer Academic Publishers
101 Philip Drive
Assinippi Park
Norwell, Massachusetts 02061 USA
Telephone (781) 871-6600
Fax (781) 871-6528
E-Mail <kluwer@wkap.com>

**Distributors for all other countries:**
Kluwer Academic Publishers Group
Distribution Centre
Post Office Box 322
3300 AH Dordrecht, THE NETHERLANDS
Telephone 31 78 6392 392
Fax 31 78 6546 474
E-Mail <orderdept@wkap.nl>

Electronic Services <http://www.wkap.nl>

**Library of Congress Cataloging-in-Publication Data**

Ontologies and databases / edited by Athman Bouguettaya.
p. cm.
"A Special issue of Distributed and parallel databases, an international journal, volume 7, no. 1 (1999)."
Includes bibliographical references and index.
ISBN 978-1-4419-5073-4
1. Database management. 2. Distributed databases. 3. Parallel processing (Electronic computers) I. Bouguettaya, Athman. II. Distributed and parallel databases.
QA76.9.D3058 1999
005.74--dc21 98-49398
CIP



*Printed on acid-free paper.*

Distributed and Parallel Databases, 7, 5–6 (1999)


# Guest Editor's Introduction

As a result of the popular deployment of the Internet and Web, one of the most vexing technological problems of the information age is about to be solved: worldwide information connectivity. Ironically, this has led to the emergence of new problems that were previously pushed aside because of a lack of cheaply available connectivity. In that regard, the age old goal of "information at our fingertips" remains largely just that, a goal. This is especially true when applied to sharing *useful* information, i.e., data stored in corporate databases. However, active research in different areas of databases are making that goal closer to being achieved.

The true benefits of using the Internet and the Web will certainly come from the ability to seamlessly interoperate systems despite their different platforms, languages, protocols and physical locations. Because connectivity is no longer considered an issue, the challenge is now on providing an infrastructure that will allow the dynamic formation of cooperative entities on the Web. The outcome of such an endeavor will have a tremendous impact on the way common problems are solved, business is conducted, and corporations are managed and run.

Of particular interest is the issue of the use of databases over the Web. Because mission critical data is usually stored in databases, there is a special need to address the problems of making databases cooperate efficiently on the Web to support both Internet and Intranet type of applications. Because of a lack of Web-based support for cooperative data sharing, *single* database access is typically performed through some form of CGI scripts that only allow specific operations to be performed. Because databases are typically managed by autonomous organizations, and hence developed to address specific applications, they tend to be *heterogeneous*. This essentially points to the need to define some sort of *common* understanding how the data is to be *presented* and *understood*.

Because of the sheer size of the Web, the data volume is steadily becoming larger, formats of data repositories are getting more diverse, and the information space is increasingly dynamic. In light of these developments, one emerging area that holds promise to define a common representation and understanding is the use of *ontologies* in databases. It is currently an active research area that draws from well established disciplines like AI, linguistics, and philosophy. Researchers in databases are now discovering the merits of using ontologies in light of the exploding domain applications made possible by the worldwide deployment of the Internet and the WWW. One such application has been the use of ontologies to encode users' contexts and domain-specific knowledge about information sources that are most likely relevant to various disciplines or subjects. Ontologies are also emerging as powerful tools for handling various aspects of information interoperation and brokering over heterogeneous digital data and services.

This special issue is a tribute to this emerging area of research. I am very pleased to present three excellent papers that were selected among a number of good submissions. They all deal with a different research aspect of the use of ontologies in the context of the wide use of databases.

The paper by A. Ouksel, "Ontologies are not the Panacea in Data Integration: A Flexible Coordinator to Mediate Context Construction", addresses the issue of semantic conflicts across databases. The driving argument behind this research is the realization that the robustness of semantic reconciliation lies with the ability for a system to be query directed. A semantic reconciliation system SCOPES (Semantic Coordinator Over parallel Exploration Spaces) is presented. SCOPES follows a non-monotonic reasoning process. A combination of a classification of conflicts, Assumption-based Truth Maintenance System (ATMS) and the Dempster-Shafer theory of belief are used to model the likelihood of assertions.

The paper by L. Liu *al*, "Controlled Vocabularies in OODBs: Modeling Issues and Implementation", proposes a technique to represent semantic network-based *controlled vocabularies* (CVs) as object-oriented databases. For that purpose, a formalization of structural concepts within semantic networks is used to disambiguate the process of mapping to object-oriented databases. A program to map a semantic network to an object-oriented schema is then described. Two CVs from the medical field are used as a proof of concept.

The paper by S. Castano and V. de Antonellis, "A discovery-based Approach to Database Ontology Design", addresses the discovery of ontologies from database schemas. The two-stage discovery approach for database ontology design is based on the classification and unification stages. In the classification stage, clusters of schema elements that are semantically similar are constructed. In the unification stage, ontology concepts from clusters of similar elements are then extracted. The authors provide the theoretical foundations for the two stages. The discovery techniques are further illustrated by the use of an application.

Finally, I would like to thank all the referees who did a tremendous job reviewing the papers in a relatively short period of time. I would also like to thank all the authors for considering this special issue as an outlet for their research. Special thanks to Mourad Ouzzani for all the help with the review process logistics.

**Athman Bouguettaya**
**Editorial Board Member**

Distributed and Parallel Databases 7, 7–35 (1999)


# Ontologies are not the Panacea in Data Integration: A Flexible Coordinator to Mediate Context Construction

ARIS M. OUKSEL aris@uic.edu
IQBAL AHMED
*The University of Illinois at Chicago, Department of Information and Decision Sciences (M/C 294), Chicago, IL 60607*

**Recommended by:** Athman Bouguettaya

**Abstract.** Shared ontologies describe concepts and relationships to resolve semantic conflicts amongst users accessing multiple autonomous and heterogeneous information sources. We contend that while ontologies are useful in semantic reconciliation, they do not guarantee correct classification of semantic conflicts, nor do they provide the capability to handle evolving semantics or a mechanism to support a dynamic reconciliation process. Their limitations are illustrated through a conceptual analysis of several prominent examples used in heterogeneous database systems and in natural language processing. We view semantic reconciliation as a nonmonotonic query-dependent process that requires flexible interpretation of query context, and as a mechanism to coordinate knowledge elicitation while constructing the query context. We propose a system that is based on these characteristics, namely the SCOPES (Semantic Coordinator Over Parallel Exploration Spaces) system. SCOPES takes advantage of ontologies to constrain exploration of a remote database during the incremental discovery and refinement of the context within which a query can be answered. It uses an Assumption-based Truth Maintenance System (ATMS) to manage the multiple plausible contexts which coexist while the semantic reconciliation process is unfolding, and the Dempster-Shafer (DS) theory of belief to model the likelihood of these plausible contexts.

**Keywords:** ontology, semantic reconciliation, heterogeneous database systems, heterogeneous information systems, semantic interoperability, data integration, semantic conflicts

## 1. Introduction

Organizations have witnessed an increasing demand for access to data obtained from multiple information systems to support operational control and decision making requirements. In this environment, the ability to effectively integrate data has a direct impact on the organizational performance. If the various information systems have been developed independently, they are likely to be semantically heterogeneous, in that, they differ in logical interpretations of data and domains captured by each system, in structural representations, in data models, and in naming and format specifications of data. A central problem of data integration is the design of mechanisms to resolve these semantic conflicts.

Several approaches [1, 2, 4, 6, 7, 19, 27], each with severe limitations, have been proposed in the past to deal with semantic conflicts. The most recent one, and arguably the most popular, is based on the use of a shared ontology, which is defined as a description of concepts and the relationships that can exist for an agent or a “community of agents” [6]. An ontology specifies a vocabulary to enable mutual understanding among its users as they adopt it to describe and to interpret shared information [5–7, 19]. For example, consider the following portion of the **Time** section from the Planning Ontology Initiative in the ARPA/Rome Laboratory Planning Initiative (ARPI) [26].

| | Time |
|---|---|
| Duration | (Infinity, Epsilon, Zero, years, weeks, days, hours, minutes) |
| Duration-bounds | (min-duration, max-duration) |
| Time-point | (Date (Origin, Offset) |
| | (Calendar-date (year, month, day, hour, minute)) |
| | pt-distance (pt<, pt<=, pt>, pt>, pt>=, pt=)) |
| Time-interval | (Always, interval-begin, interval-end, min-duration, max-duration, interval-before) |

The resolution of semantic conflicts using ontology is a three-step process [6]. First, a shared ontology is defined; second, objects from cooperating information systems are described using the ontology, and third, the similarity between different objects is determined via the ontology. For example, consider objects **periodicity**, and **time-factor** which exists in two financial databases DB1 and DB2, respectively. Assume that instances of ‘periodicity’ in DB1 represent the number of days for which a stock is associated with a particular risk factor (e.g., an instance ‘4’ of ‘periodicity’ refers to four days), while the instances of ‘time-factor’ in DB2 represent the time period in hours during which a stock is associated with a particular risk factor (e.g., an instance ‘4’ of ‘time-factor’ refers to a 4 hour period). On the basis of an *ontological commitment*, which is an agreement to use a vocabulary (i.e., ask queries and make assertions) in a way that is consistent with respect to the theory specified by an ontology [5], database administrators (DBAs) of these databases can map the objects ‘periodicity’ and ‘time-factor’ from their respective databases to the common concept **duration** in the ontology. A further mapping of ‘periodicity’ and ‘time-factor’ to *days* and *hours* respectively (both are also concepts present in the ontology) will ensure that an accurate semantic interpretation of these concepts is represented in the ontology. The ontology is then used to ascertain that object ‘periodicity’ and object ‘time-factor’ from DB1 and DB2 are semantically related.

Several promising semantic reconciliation approaches including the Concept Hierarchy Model (CHM) [27], the Summary Schema Model (SSM) [2], the Semantic Proximity Model (SemPro) [7], and the Context Interchange Network (COIN) [4, 19] are based on the ontology approach. SSM and CHM use the terms ‘summary schema’ and ‘concept hierarchy’, respectively, to describe those data structures used for reconciling semantic conflicts. According to the definition of ontology, both these data structures could be classified as ontologies. The concept hierarchy in CHM could in fact be categorized as a domain specific ontology.

The general assumption is that the ontology approach significantly reduces the complexity of determining similarity between different *objects* from Heterogeneous Information

Sources (HIS). This assumption is mainly justified on the basis of the criteria used to design ontologies [25]: (a) *Clarity*; the intent of the terms in an ontology is clear and there is minimal ambiguity amongst terms, (b) *Coherence*; the ontology is internally consistent, (c) *Extensibility*; the design of an ontology ensures that additional specialized terms can be added to the existing vocabulary without mandating an alteration of existing definitions, (d) *Minimal Encoding Bias*; the ontology is implemented to permit knowledge sharing across agents that may be implemented using different representation systems and styles, and finally, (e) *Ontological Commitment*; the ontology mandates the minimal ontological commitment required to facilitate the intended knowledge sharing exercise. It is our contention that ontology-based reconciliation suffers from the same kind of drawbacks as the global schema approaches [2, 6–8, 18], even if the above design criteria are actually satisfied. Specifically:

(a) It is neither practical nor theoretically possible to develop and maintain an ontology that strictly adheres to the design criteria specified above, particularly in an environment of evolving semantics [24].
(b) An ontology does not identify and classify semantic conflicts accurately.
(c) An ontology cannot handle query-directed reconciliation, which requires multiple interpretations of semantic conflicts.
(d) An ontology does not provide the coordination mechanism to discover metadata knowledge for semantic reconciliation, and to ensure consistency across all the mappings relevant to a query.

We illustrate these limitations through a conceptual analysis of two promising ontology-based semantic reconciliation techniques, namely COIN [4, 19] and SemPro [7]. Despite their drawbacks, ontologies are very useful in semantic reconciliation when their application is properly circumscribed. For example, they can serve to establish initial mappings, referred heretofore as **anchors**, between terms of a local and a remote information system. These initial mappings are necessary to constrain the propagation of search for the correct query-dependent semantic reconciliation between terms. In this paper, we assume that semantic reconciliation is generally context-dependent, and the set of interpretations is not commensurable, as is usually the case in most interesting applications. Therefore, interpretations of concepts, or across a multiplicity of concepts cannot be fixed a priori. We describe a semantic reconciliation system which circumvents the limitations of ontologies listed above, namely SCOPES (Semantic Coordinator Over Parallel Exploration Spaces) [18], and yet exploits their capabilities to initialize construction of the *context* used for reconciliation. **MIKROKOSMOS** [9, 10, 12], an ontology currently available online on the World Wide Web, is used for illustration.

In SCOPES, semantic reconciliation is a nonmonotonic reasoning process, where inter-schema mappings asserted at one point may be corroborated or retracted as further supporting or contradictory evidence is uncovered. Ontologies can be used to constrain exploration of a remote database during the incremental discovery and refinement process of the *context* within which a query to a remote database can be answered. The management of these multiple, often contradictory and yet plausible set of assertions is supported in SCOPES by using an Assumption Based Truth Maintenance System (ATMS) [3]. The

Dempster-Shafer (DS) theory of belief [20] is used in conjunction with the ATMS to model the likelihood of these plausible sets of assertions. An advantage of using ontologies, such as MIKROKOSMOS, is their provision of similarity measures that can be used to compute the measures of belief assigned to the multiple plausible contexts.

In Section 2 we describe a running example used throughout the paper. We motivate our work by proving through counter-examples the inadequacy of ontologies to deal with complex semantic reconciliation in general, and consequently justifying the design of a system like SCOPES in Section 3. In Sections 4 and 5, we give an overview of COIN and SemPro, examine why they fail to provide a solution to the problem of semantic heterogeneity, and speculate on how to increase their effectiveness in achieving semantic heterogeneity among HIS. In Section 6 we describe SCOPES, illustrate how SCOPES can overcome the drawbacks of ontologies and exploit their advantages. We conclude with a summary of results achieved and a brief list of further work.

## 2. Running example

The schemas described below will be used throughout the paper to illustrate our claims. Figure 1 is a partial schema of a database which maintains information on the Engineering Faculty of Chicago-based Universities, while figure 2 depicts a partial schema of an Employee database of Engineering-related firms. We will refer to these databases as DB1 and DB2, respectively.

- **DB1:** A database of Engineering Faculty members of Chicago-based Universities
  Data Model: Non-Normalized Relational Schema (partial), see figure 1.
- **DB2:** A database of employees of engineering-related firms
  Data Model: Non-Normalized Relational Schema (partial), see figure 2.

There exist several semantic correspondences between DB1 and DB2. First, class 'Faculty' in DB1 and class 'Employee' in DB2 intersect. Instances of attribute 'SS#' in DB1 correspond to instances of attribute 'ID' in DB2 where the employees are consultants from Chicago-based Universities. Attributes 'Dept' in DB1 and DB2 share some common domain values; as do 'Sal_Type' in DB1 and 'Comp_Type' in DB2; and 'Sal_Amt' in DB1 and 'Comp' in DB2. As we shall see later, these three pairs may be considered either as

**Faculty (<u>SS#</u>, Name, Dept, Sal_Amt, Sal _Type, Affiliation, Sponsor, University....)**

| | |
|---|---|
| *Faculty:* | *Any tuple of the relation Faculty, identified by the key SS#* |
| *SS#:* | *An identifier, the social security number of a faculty member* |
| *Name:* | *An identifier, Name of a faculty member* |
| *Dept:* | *The academic or non-academic department to which a faculty member is affiliated* |
| *Sal_Amt:* | *The amount of annual Salary paid to a Faculty member* |
| *Sal_Type:* | *The type of salary such as Base Salary, Grant, and Honorarium* |
| *Affiliation:* | *The affiliation of a faculty member, such as teaching, non-teaching, research* |
| *University:* | *The University where a Faculty member is employed* |

*Figure 1.*

**Employee (ID, Name, Type, Employer, Dept, CompType, Comp, Affiliation....)**

| | |
|---|---|
| *Employee:* | *Any tuple of the relation Employee, identified by the key ID* |
| *ID:* | *An identifier, the social security number of an Employee* |
| *Name:* | *An identifier, Name of an employee* |
| *Type:* | *An attribute describing the job category of an Employee, such as Executive, Middle Manager, Consultant from another firm, etc* |
| *Employer:* | *Name of the employer firm such as AT&T, Motorola, General Motors, etc* |
| *Dept:* | *Name of the department where an Employee works* |
| *CompType:* | *The type of compensation given to an employee, such as Base Salary, Contract Amount* |
| *Comp:* | *The amount of annual compensation for an employee* |
| *Affiliation:* | *Name of the Consultant firm, such as a University Name, Andersen Consulting, ...* |

*Figure 2.*

synonyms or as homonyms depending on the nature of the query. Attributes 'Affiliation' in DB1 and DB2 are homonyms, as are attribute 'University' in DB1 and attribute 'Employer' in DB2, because their domains do not overlap. The fact that the domains are not overlapping is simply circumstantial, and therefore it cannot be assumed a priori. The two attributes could as easily have been overlapping in other database instances.

Attribute 'University' in DB1 and 'Affiliation' in DB2 may be considered as synonyms for the subset of class 'Employee' where 'Employee.Type = Consultant' , and where the values in the domain of the attribute 'Affiliation' in DB2 correspond to the names of Chicago-based Universities. Semantic reconciliation approaches, such as COIN or SemPro, designed to identify and reconcile semantic incompatibilities, should be capable of discovering these distinctions. Yet, as we show in the next section, COIN and SemPro fail to capture the nuances necessary to properly classify the correspondences. In our view, no ontology is capable of modeling the complexity of possible semantic interpretations.

## 3. Problem motivation

Ontology-based reconciliation techniques require an ontological commitment, which implies a standardized use of concepts and a priori semantic knowledge before semantic incompatibilities can be resolved. We believe it is this standardization which limits the usability of the ontology approach. By statically fixing semantic interpretation as is done in a global schema approach, ontologies do not provide the flexibility necessary to handle query dependent integration between autonomously and independently designed information systems. For example, the terms 'University' and 'Employer' from DB1 and DB2, respectively, may both be mapped to a common concept **Employer** in an ontology. Thus, per the ontology, we may assert that these terms are synonyms. The assertion is true if a query: Q: "*List Names of Employers of Engineering Related Professionals*" is posed against the two databases. But if a query: Q′: "*List Names of Academic Institutions*" is posed instead, the synonymy relation between the two terms no longer holds, and its assumption will produce erroneous results.

Terms 'affiliation' and 'affiliation' from DB1 and DB2, respectively, may be mapped to a term **Affiliation** in the ontology, thus asserting that these two terms are synonymous. This assertion is incorrect since the attributes corresponding to these two terms in DB1 and DB2 have different domain values, the synonymy relation asserted by the ontology is incorrect.

A cursory analysis of the schemas described in figures 1 and 2 reveals that term 'affiliation' in DB2 has a synonymy relationship with 'University' in DB1, instead. As it were, this latter correspondence will not emerge in an ontology-based semantic reconciliation process, because it will be pair (University, Employer) that will map to the same concept in a general ontology. One may speculate as to the possibility of constructing an ontology specifically designed to handle semantic reconciliation amongst DB1 and DB2. The pair (affiliation, university) may then be mapped to the same concept. This ontology may not show a synonymy relationship between the two terms 'affiliation'. But, clearly, this obviates the generality and the flexibility of the semantic reconciliation autonomy of the two procedures, and imposes stringent restrictions on the two databases akin to a global schema approach. In addition to the impracticality of such an approach, the autonomy of databases is also violated.

One other way is to assume that the ontologies are designed autonomously. The semantic conflicts may then be resolved by composing the two ontologies. But composition of ontologies is also a complex semantic reconciliation problem. Furthermore, it has to be done dynamically each time a query is posed, otherwise it may suffer from the same problems as a global schema approach.

Another example is that of the generalization/specialization relationship between (Faculty, Employee) pair. Ontologies are useless in this case, since they can at best provide a similarity mapping between the terms without specifically identifying the exact nature of the semantic conflict, i.e., the generalization/specialization abstraction.

Reconciliation techniques such as COIN and SemPro attempt to resolve the semantic conflicts existing at the schema level by providing a standardized description of schema level objects at a higher level of abstraction, i.e., the *metaattribute* level. The metaattributes are additional concepts that explicitly specify the various semantic explications of the schema level objects [4, 7, 19]. The assumption underlying this approach is that semantic conflicts may occur only at the schema level and not at the metaattribute level, implying that:

1. There is a complete and universal agreement about the meaning and use of metaattributes across the network [24].
2. Data Base Administrators (DBAs) know a priori all possible contexts in which their database can be queried. As a result they specify at the outset all possible properties and their possible values for each attribute in their local schemas.

The first assumption suggests that even though different DBAs may assign different names to the schema level objects representing the same real-world objects, any particular property or characteristic of these objects is well understood in a standardized manner across any large network, will not change over time, and is universally mapped to the same concept(s) in the ontology by DBAs across the network. The approach overlooks the fact that it is the difference in perspectives of the same DBAs that is a major cause of the existence of semantic conflicts in the first place. The result is creating a structure similar to the global schema with the difference that semantics are now being 'fixed' at one higher level of abstraction, i.e., the metaattribute level instead of the schema level. Additionally, as shown above for the attributes *Affiliation* of DB1 and DB2, the values assigned to these metaattributes also represent real-life concepts, and unless these are 'fixed', also are susceptible to the same kind of semantic conflicts faced at the schema level.

The effect of the second assumption is again the creation of a structure akin to that in a global schema. For example, the DBA of DB2 may not explicitly associate concept *research* as a metaattribute the concept 'Employee', some instances of which also represent in DB2 the academics working for the company as consultants. Hence, a query posed against DB1 and DB2 inquiring about a list of researchers may not be answerable unless the DBA of DB2 knows a priori that such an information request may be of interest to someone in the network, and in anticipation of such a query associates concept *research* with concept *Employee* well in advance. Several researchers [7, 16, 18] have contended that this second assumption is stringent in most practical situations, since a priori inventory of all the possible ways a database may be queried is totally unrealistic.

The strength of a dynamic semantic reconciliation approach lies in its extensibility, scalability, and its capability of dealing with evolving semantics [4, 18]. It should be able to:

- identify and classify all semantic conflicts;
- support flexible query-dependent interpretation of semantic conflicts;
- support discovery and reconciliation of semantic conflicts in an environment of incomplete and uncertain semantic knowledge;
- support the coexistence of multiple plausible contexts during the reconciliation process; and
- support a query-directed coordination mechanism for the dynamic elicitation of semantic knowledge.

SCOPES possesses all the characteristics listed above. The same cannot be said of ontology-based approaches. Using two specific ontologies, namely COIN and SemPro, and a few counter-examples, we prove our claim. A detailed analysis of other ontology-based approaches is given in [15, 16].

## 4. Context interchange network

### 4.1. *Brief description*

The Context Interchange Network (COIN) [4, 19] is an approach which attempts to resolve the semantic heterogeneity problem by enumerating additional standardized terms, taken from a shared ontology, to describe the semantics of schema level terms. A context mediator is responsible for matching terms from different databases and resolving any remaining conflicts. The mediator in COIN is based on Wiederhold's context mediator concept [23], and utilizes a theory of *semantic values* as a unit of data exchange among heterogeneous information systems (HIS). A **semantic value** is defined as a simple value combined with its related context, where a simple datum is an instance of a type; and the context of a simple value is defined as the associated metadata relating to its meaning, properties (such as source, quality, precision etc.), and organization. For example, consider the attribute 'Sal_Amt'

*Create table* ***Faculty***

| | |
|---|---|
| *(SS#* | *char (11)* |
| *Name* | *char (40)* |
| *Dept* | *char (25) (Chairperson char (40), Size int, Budget float (Currency char (4), Scale factor int))* |
| *Sal-Amt* | *float (Currency char (9), Scale factor int, Type char (20))* |
| *Affiliation* | *char (20)* |
| *Sponsor* | *char (50) (Grant float (Currency char (4), Scale-factor int, term char (10)), Dept char (25))* |
| *University* | *char (60) (President char (40), Size int, Annual Budget float (Currency char (4), Scale factor int))* |

*Create table* ***Employee***

| | |
|---|---|
| *(ID* | *char (9)(Type char (10))* |
| *Employer* | *char (15) (Head office char (40), Size int, Annual Budget float (Currency char (4), Scale factor int))* |
| *Name* | *char (38)* |
| *Dept* | *char (20)(Head char (38), Size int, Dept Code char (5), Location char (35))* |
| *Comp* | *float (Type char (6), Currency char (9), Scale factor int)* |
| *Affiliation* | *char (40) (title char (10), Head char (40), Size int)* |

**An example of the semantic value schemata for the above relations as defined by a predicate is given as:**

*Create scene for Faculty and Employee by predicates: Currency = 'dollars' and scale-factor = '1000'*

*Figure 3.*

from DB1 that appears as a simple value '80' in the database. The context of this simple value will be metadata such as its currency, scale factor, periodicity, etc. Its semantic value can be written as '80' (currency = 'dollars', scale factor = '1000', periodicity = 'yearly', type = 'base salary'), where 'currency', 'scale-factor', 'periodicity', and 'type' are relevant concepts derived from the associated metadata. The terms 'dollars', '1000', 'yearly', 'base salary' are the values assigned to metaattributes.

For the relational model the semantic values are modeled as a sub-tuple of the simple values. Each property of the semantic value corresponds to an attribute in the sub-tuple. These attributes are called *metaattributes*. The attributes present in the base tuple are called *base attributes*. For example, the attribute 'Sal_Amt' in figure 3 is a base attribute, whereas 'currency', 'scale factor', 'periodicity', and 'type' are metaattributes.

An example of **data environment** is illustrated in figure 3. These environments are created in accordance with a shared ontology to associate the relevant context with the simple values. The data environments consist of two components namely the *semantic-value schema*; which is a declaration of the properties associated with each semantic value, and the *semantic-value schemata*; which specifies values for these properties.

### 4.2. *Limitations of the COIN approach*

COIN has been called a dynamic integration approach in [4, 19]. Yet, as we show in the next subsections, a few counter-examples demonstrate that, despite reliance on a shared-ontology, COIN does not exhibit the characteristics of a truly dynamic approach. Let us consider the example in figure 4.

***4.2.1. COIN is limited in its identification and classification of semantic conflicts.*** Consider the example in figure 4, where Q1 posed against DB1 is to be translated into a query Q2 against DB2. To construct Q2, COIN must find in DB2 the semantic entities corresponding to terms 'SS#', 'Faculty', 'Sponsor', and 'University' in Q1. Assume the ontology yields

Consider Q1 posed against DB1, and Q2 it's semantically equivalent translation posed against DB2.
*Q1: 'List those 'UIC' faculty members who are consultants at Motorola'*
**Q1: Select** SS# **From** Faculty **Where** Sponsor = 'Motorola' **and** University ='UIC'
**Q1': Select** ID **From** Employee **Where** Employer in ('Motorola', 'UIC')
**Q2: Select** ID **From** Employee **Where** Employee.type ='CONSULTANT' **and** Affiliation = 'UIC' **and** Employer ='Motorola'

*Figure 4.*

the following most likely synonymy correspondences: (SS#, ID), (Faculty, Employee), (Sponsor, Employer), (University, Employer) between the terms in Q1 and terms in DB2, respectively. Query Q1 can then be simply erroneously translated to Q1′. At this point, the context mediator does not possess sufficient intelligence to validate, refute, or refine the correspondences simultaneously across all terms asserted by the ontology, or to further investigate other correspondences, such as (University, Affiliation) pair, for an accurate translation of Q1 to Q2. The mediator has no mechanism to recover from initial plausible, yet incorrect, mappings. For all purposes, the process stops.

***4.2.2. COIN lacks flexibility to interpret the query context.*** An advantage of COIN over traditional static integration approaches is its capability to support multiple contexts by using metaattributes. Still, the DBA's perspective and the ontology impose a priori the possible interpretations allowed. As a result, there are valid queries that cannot be handled. For example, consider the contradictory interpretations required by queries Q and Q′ as discussed in Section 3. COIN does not provide the flexibility to dynamically select the appropriate interpretation depending on the specific query, and thereby allow both Q and Q′ to be answered. The metaattributes of (University, Employer) pair are defined similarly in both databases. Hence, regardless of the context of a given query, such as Q′, the context mediator has no mechanism to refute the initial synonymy correspondence provided by the ontology.

***4.2.3. COIN lacks any coordination mechanism.*** There are several possible semantic mappings between attributes 'SS#' in DB1 and 'ID' in DB2. The correct correspondence cannot be ascertained by confining the process of disambiguation to evidence directly tied to these two attributes only. Disambiguation in this case would require enlarging the investigation scope to the whole schematic environment to gain a better perspective. For example, the investigation could be pursued by examining the correspondence between objects 'Faculty' and 'Employee' to which the two attributes belong, or by looking at their instances. We refer to these investigation as "upward propagation" or "downward propagation", respectively. The ontology may be used to assign an initial mapping. Let us assume that objects 'Faculty' and 'Employee' are found to be homonyms or unrelated, the initial correspondence between 'SS#' and 'ID' must be revised as unrelated, and further knowledge should be elicited to discover other mappings to DB2. Similarly, refuting the synonymy relationship in pair ('University', 'Employer') may only be achieved by examining specific instances. For example, by determining that value 'UIC' of 'University' does not exist in the domain of 'Employer', the synonymy mapping is rejected. Note that the exact nature of the relationship between the domains is unnecessary for the query at hand. The disambiguation process is query-specific.

The two examples above clearly illustrate the necessity for a systematic coordination mechanism capable of managing the multiple plausible contexts that may coexist at any one point in time during the semantic reconciliation process in environment with incomplete and uncertain knowledge; of eliciting further evidence for their corroboration (refutation); and of updating the plausibility of these contexts as a result of knowledge discovery. COIN does not provide or support such coordination, and therefore is limited in its capability to deal with semantic interoperability amongst HIS.

## 5. The semantic proximity model

### 5.1. *Brief description of SemPro*

SemPro [7] attempts to capture the various semantic interpretations of a schema object by specifying additional descriptive terms taken from a shared ontology. A collection of these terms is considered as the context of an object. The representation of context in the SemPro model is of the general form:

$$\text{Context} = \langle (C_1, V_1)(C_2, V_2) \ldots (C_k, V_k) \rangle$$

Each $C_i$, where $1 \leq i \leq k$, is a contextual coordinate denoting an aspect of context. It may model some characteristic of the subject domain and can be obtained from a shared ontology; it may model an implicit assumption in the design of a database. And it may or may not be associated with an attribute $A_j$ of an object O. Each $V_i$, where $1 \leq i \leq k$, can be a variable; it can be a set; it can be a variable associated with a context; and it can be a set associated with a context.

SemPro provides a mechanism for comparison and manipulation of different contexts, such as the context of a query and the definition context of an object. This mechanism is based on the specificity relationship between two contexts, which is defined as 'given two contexts $C_1$ and $C_2$, $C_1 \leq C_2$ iff $C_1$ is at least as specific as $C_2$. The specificity relationship induces a partial order such that a greatest lower bound (*glb*) exists for any two contexts thus leading to the organization of the context set as a meet semilattice. The glb (or the least common denominator in this case) of two contexts is defined as 'the most specific context which is more general than either of the two contexts.'

The representations in figures 5 and 6 are in accordance with the SemPro model of context. For example, in figure 5 the terms identifier, department, employer, sponsor,

**Representation of Definition Context for Faculty and Employee Schemas**

Faculty$_{def}$ :< (identifier, {name, SS#}), (department,{DEPARTMENT}),
(reimbursement, {salary, honorarium, grant}), (affiliation, {research, teaching, non-teaching}
(employer, X o {UNIVERSITY}),(sponsor, {AT&T, Motorola, GM,....})>

Employee$_{def}$ :< (identifier, {name, ID}), (Department, {DEPARTMENT}),(employer, {Motorola}),
(category, {Exec, MidMgr, CONSULTANT o <(affiliation, {firmname})>}),
(reimbursement, {Salary,Contract Amt.})>

*Figure 5.*

**Representation of Q1's Definition Context**

$Q_{def}$: < (identifier, SS#), (sponsor, Motorola), (employer, UIC), (Faculty, FACULTY) >

*Figure 6.*

reimbursement, category, affiliation are contextual coordinates. The terms in brackets are specified values for these contextual coordinates. '*X*' is a variable. UNIVERSITY and DEPARTMENT are objects. *X* ∘ {UNIVERSITY} denotes that *X* can take its values from the set of Universities. CONSULTANT is an object that is a subset of EMPLOYEE and has a contextual coordinate 'affiliation'.

## 5.2. *Drawbacks of the SemPro approach*

The intent of the above representation is to anticipate the likely mappings between different databases. The goal is to a priori circumscribe the set of possible contexts within which queries may be translated. The most specific context for a given query is then obtained by computing the 'glb' of the database context and the query context. The correlation of semantically related concepts in the resulting 'glb' is determined via an ontology. This approach may be efficient in limited application domains, since the set of contexts is finite. But, it is not adequate to deal with semantic conflicts in a dynamic environment with autonomous information sources. Basically the same conflicts as may have existed at the schema level have not been eliminated.

Consider the context definition for DB2 given by $Employee_{def}$ in figure 5, and that for Q1 given by $Q_{def}$ in figure 6. Consider once again mapping Q1, posed against DB1, to a semantically equivalent query against DB2. Figure 7(a) shows the resulting context, hereby referred to as $C_{glb}$. It was obtained using SemPro rules [7] for computing the glb of any two contexts. Figure 7(b) shows the context representation of the target query Q2 against DB2.

$C_{glb}$ contains the knowledge that is required to translate Q1 to Q2. However, this translation can be obtained only if correct correspondences between DB1 and DB2 have been already determined. It is evident that due to the limitations already mentioned in the sections above, the *more general context* given by $C_{glb}$ does not accurately identify all the

$C_{glb}$ = glb ($Employee_{def}$, $Q_{def}$) :
<(identifier, {SS#}), (Department, {DEPARTMENT}),(employer, glb{Motorola, UIC}),(category, {Exec, MidMgr., CONSULTANT o <(affiliation, glb{firmname, research, teaching, non teaching})>}), (reimbursement, glb{Salary, Contract-Amt, grant }), (sponsor, Motorola), (Faculty, FACULTY) >

(a)

$Q2_{def}$: <(identifier, {ID),(employer, {Motorola}), (category, {CONSULTANT o <(affiliation, {UIC})>}),>

(b)

*Figure 7.*

correspondences nor does it provide the refinement process that can lead to a representation such as $Q2_{def}$.

In SemPro, it is assumed that all semantic interpretations of an object can be represented explicitly, thus ensuring the availability of all metadata knowledge needed for semantic reconciliation. While this is already questionable, it is precisely the discovery of these semantic interpretations that makes the problem of reconciliation very complex. For example, assuming $C_{glb}$ contains within it the knowledge to translate Q1. There is no indication on how to discover this knowledge. SemPro does not provide a coordination mechanism that can be applied systematically to refine this context and to determine the precise knowledge, which is required to translate Q1 to Q2.

## 6. Semantic coordinator over parallel exploration spaces (SCOPES)

### 6.1. *Lessons from COIN and SemPro*

Both COIN and SemPro are useful to find anchors or points of reference in a remote database using ontology. These anchors are basically plausible mappings that are used to trigger further exploration of the remote database to ascertain the validity of these initial mappings or, if refuted, to discover new stronger mappings. Anchors serve as starting points for semantic reconciliation. The examples discussed above clearly illustrate the limitations of COIN and SemPro that impede the semantic reconciliation process in a dynamic environment. The mediation is highly dependent on a priori semantic knowledge, whose availability is unlikely in most practical situations. COIN and SemPro have an advantage over the global schema approach in that several plausible contexts are allowed to coexist, although one might argue that this is also possible in the global schema approach. The assumption is that these contexts can be defined a priori. But they do not display the flexibility to handle unanticipated queries and contexts in a dynamic environment as is likely to happen on the web or in intranets or extranets. Their dependency on the standardized use of concepts across a large network of databases is also unreasonable. The resolution of semantic conflicts mandates incrementally uncovering and piecing together the view of a remote schema, which is pertinent to answering a specific query [18].

### 6.2. *Brief overview of the SCOPES approach*

SCOPES [18] is an architecture, which facilitates incremental construction of the context within which meaningful exchange of information between HIS can take place. It supports semantic reconciliation under partial semantic knowledge, by coordinating query directed elicitation of information. Knowledge acquisition exploits available reconciliation techniques and other knowledge sources. Since the incremental system makes assertions under partial knowledge, the knowledge acquisition process may generate multiple plausible contexts, each of which needs to be corroborated through the acquisition of additional supporting evidence. The SCOPES approach incrementally uncovers and assembles together the specific view of another schema which is pertinent to answering a specific query. In our view, semantic reconciliation is a nonmonotonic reasoning process, where schematic mappings which are asserted at one point in reconciliation may be retracted after eliciting further evidence. In SCOPES the ATMS is used in conjunction with the Dempster-Schafer theory of belief for the representation and resolution of ambiguity.

### 6.3. *Conceptual components used in SCOPES*

***6.3.1. Classification of semantic conflicts.*** Semantic conflicts between heterogeneous conceptual schemas arise due to differences in data models, differences in logical interpretation of data captured by each system, different structural representations, mismatched domains, and different naming and formatting schemes employed by the individual systems. We briefly describe below the classification of semantic conflicts [14] used in SCOPES.

Semantic conflicts are classified along three dimensions namely, *naming*, *abstraction*, and *levels of heterogeneity*. The Inter-Schema Correspondence Assertion (ISCA) which represents the semantic relationship between two elements of different databases has the general form:

Assert[naming, abstraction, heterogeneity]

where *naming* (*abstraction*) stands for a naming (abstraction) function between an element $x$ in the local database and an element $y$ in either the local or the remote database; heterogeneity indicates the structural schema description of $x$ and $y$ in their respective databases. This classification combines the dimensions of semantic conflicts with a structural description, the heterogeneity dimension, thereby facilitating the process of operational integration.

Along the dimension of naming, the relationships between two elements $x$ and $y$ can be categorized as *synonyms*, denoted $syn(x, y)$, which are terms having similar meaning; *homonyms*, denoted $hom(x, y)$, which are similar terms representing different concepts; and *unrelated* , denoted $unrel(x, y)$, which are not related along the dimension of naming; however, these could be related in some other way such as functional relationships. Along the dimension of abstraction, the relationships between two elements $x$ and $y$ can be categorized as *class* relationship, denoted $class(x, y)$; *generalization/specialization* relationship, $gen(x, y)$; *aggregation* relationships, denoted $agg(x, y)$; and relationships due to *computed* or *derived functions*, denoted *function-name*$(x, y)$. The levels of heterogeneity include the *object* level, the *attribute* level and the *instance* level of the database schema. Semantic conflicts due to naming and abstraction can occur at any of these levels within the same or two different databases. Thus this level provides us with a structural mapping between two corresponding elements from different databases. This dimension requires a pair of values, one for each element $x$ and $y$, as represented in its corresponding schema. Each value is denoted either $att(x, O, DB)$, where $x$ is the element considered in the assertion, $O$ is the class of objects to which it is attributed, $DB$ the database in which it appears; or $obj(x, DB)$, where $x$ is a class in $DB$; $inst(x, O, DB)$, where $x$ is an instance of class $O$ in $DB$. (Note: when there is no ambiguity, we shall use the terms 'object' and 'class' interchangeably.)

The most important advantage of this classification is the partitioning of semantic conflicts into 12 disjoint classes based on the dimensions of naming and abstraction. Some of these classes are transient because they are valid only in the dynamic reconciliation environment, where they represent semantic conflicts which are classified in the presence of incomplete semantic knowledge, whereas the other classes are valid in both the static and the dynamic reconciliation environment. These disjoint classes are described in more detail in [14], where it is shown that the classification captures all semantic conflicts discussed in the literature on heterogeneous conceptual schemas.

***6.3.2. Managing uncertainty and incompleteness.*** Consider again the example in figure 4. The translation of Q1 to Q2 requires mapping concepts 'SS#', 'Faculty', 'Sponsor', 'University', 'UIC', and 'Motorola' of DB1 to their equivalent ones in DB2. Let us now proceed to map the terms in query Q1 to their corresponding ones in DB2. Our first concern is to find **anchors** for the query terms in DB2. An ontology can play an important role in this process. Assuming that the concepts from both databases have been translated by their local DBAs to equivalent ones in the ontology, we can get an equivalence mapping via the ontology between the attribute 'SS#' of DB1 and 'ID' of DB2. Note that the mapping of local schema terms by the DBAs to concepts in the ontology are only initial, plausible mappings. SCOPES is capable of backtracking from an incorrect interpretation, as new evidence contradicting the initial mapping is discovered. An advantage of the SCOPES approach is that it provides a recovery mechanism in case any of the initially assumed mappings are incorrect with respect to the query's context.

Without any further knowledge about the interoperating databases, any of the $2^{12}$ subsets of assertions obtained from the set of 12 possible assertions is an equally valid context. To refine this set of assertions, further correspondences, such as the one between the objects 'Faculty' and 'Employee', to which the two attributes 'SS#' and 'ID' respectively belong, needs to be asserted. According to the context of the above query and in accordance with information available from the data dictionary in Section 2 , these pairs ought to be reconciled as synonyms where *Employee.Type* = *Consultant* and *Employee.Affiliation* = *UIC*. Our intent is to illustrate how the classification of semantic conflicts described in the previous section, an ATMS, and a judicious use of an ontology, such as MIKROKOSMOS, are integrated in SCOPES to arrive at such conclusion. We use the DS theory of belief in conjunction with an ATMS to refine the context by corroborating and retracting our assertions as further evidence is collected, and to model the likelihood of these sets of assertions. We describe the salient features of the DS theory in the section below.

*6.3.2.1. Models used for plausible semantic reconciliation.* Given two elements from two different databases, there are 12 possible ISCAs based on the two dimensions of naming and abstraction. Let this set of assertions be $\Omega$. There are $2^{12}$ possible subsets of $\Omega$ represented by the power set $P(\Omega)$. Recall that in SCOPES context is described as a set of plausible ISCAs. To represent an uncertain context, for example, the context representing the mapping between terms 'SS#' from DB1 and 'ID' from DB2 with respect to a query Q1, we use the DS theory to assign portions of belief committed to the subsets of $\Omega$. The DS theory of belief is formulated in terms of a function:

$$m : P(\Omega) \rightarrow [0, 1] \quad \text{st: } m(\phi) = 0 \text{ and } \sum_{A \subseteq \Omega} m(A) = 1$$

The function $m$ is referred to as a *mass function* or a *basic probability assignment*; every subset of the environment that has a mass value greater than 0 is called a focal element. Assume that while investigating a possible mapping between terms 'SS#' from DB1 and 'ID' from DB2, evidence E provides support for the following assertions:

A1: Assert[syn(SS#, ID), class(SS#, ID), (att(SS#, Faculty, DB1), att(ID, Employee, DB2))]
A2: Assert[syn(SS#, ID), gen(SS#, ID), (att(SS#, Faculty, DB1), att(ID, Employee, DB2))]
A3: Assert[syn(SS#, ID), agg(SS#, ID), (att(SS#, Faculty, DB1), att(ID, Employee, DB2))]

Let a mass function assign a value of 0.4 to the set {A1, A2} and 0.4 to the set {A3}. The left over mass value is assigned to the larger set $\Omega\,(m(\Omega) = 0.2)$ denoting that there may be additional conditions beyond evidence E which are true with some degrees of belief.

*Definition (Evidence Set).* Let $\Omega$ be the domain of values for a set of ISCAs. Evidence set (ES) is a collection of subsets of $\Omega$ associated with mass function assignments.

For example, in the above case $ES_1 = [\{A1, A2\}^{0.4}, \{A3\}^{0.4}, \Omega^{0.2}]$ is an evidence set.

*Definition (Belief Function).* A belief function, denoted by *Bel*, corresponding to a specific mass function $m$, assigns to every subset $A$ of $\Omega$ the sum of beliefs committed exactly to every subset of $A$ by $m$, i.e.,

$$Bel(A) = \sum_{X \subseteq A} m(X). \tag{1}$$

For example,

$$\begin{aligned} Bel\{A1, A2, A3\} &= m[\{A1\}] + m[\{A2\}] + m[\{A3\}] + m[\{A1, A2\}] + m[\{A1, A3\}] \\ &\quad + m[\{A3, A2\}] + m[\{A1, A2, A3\}] \\ &= 0 + 0 + 0.4 + 0.4 + 0 + 0 + 0 = 0.8. \end{aligned}$$

The above belief function is a measure of the minimum degree of support in favor of the set {A1, A2, A3}.

*Definition (Plausibility Function).* A plausibility function, denoted by *Pls*, corresponding to a specific mass function $m$, determines the maximum belief that can be possibly contributed to a subset of $A$, i.e.,

$$Pls = 1 - Bel(A^c) \tag{2}$$

where $A^c$ is the complement of $A$ in $\Omega$, and is equivalent to $(\Omega - A)$. The plausibility function is defined to indicate the degree to which the evidence set fails to refute a subset $A$. For example,

$$Pls(\{A1, A2, A3)\} = 1 - Bel(\{A1, A2, A3\}^c) = 1 - 0 = 1.$$

The plausibility function denotes the maximum degree to which the assertion set {A1, A2, A3} cannot be disproved and hence is plausible. We can observe that by definition, $Bel(A) \leq Pls(A)$. Their difference $Pls(A) - Bel(A)$ denotes the degree to which the evidence set is uncertain whether to support $A$ or $A^c$.

**Combining evidence sets:** There may exist multiple evidence sets supporting different mass function assignments on a domain of values. Given two mass function $m_1$ and $m_2$ from two evidence sets $ES_1$ and $ES_2$, respectively, we can use the Dempster's rule of combination to combine them. The combined mass denoted by $m_1 \oplus m_2$ is defined as:

$$m_1 \oplus m_2(Z) = \sum_{Z = X \cap Y} m_1(X) \cdot m_2(Y) \tag{3}$$

For example, consider the availability of evidence set $ES_2$ which supports the following set of assertions

A1: Assert[syn(SS#, ID), class(SS#, ID), (att(SS#, Faculty, DB1), att(ID, Employee, DB2))]
A3: Assert[syn(SS#, ID), agg(SS#, ID), (att(SS#, Faculty, DB1), att(ID, Employee, DB2))]
A4: Assert[syn(SS#, ID), function(SS#, ID), (att(SS#, Faculty, DB1), att(ID, Employee, DB2))]

For clarity of expression let the mass function $m$ corresponding to $ES_1$ above be denoted as $m_1$. The mass function corresponding to $ES_2$ is denoted by $m_2$ and assigns values 0.3 to the set {A3, A4}, and 0.6 to the set {A1}. The remainder of the mass value is assigned to the larger set $\Omega\,(m(\Omega) = 0.1)$. Hence, $ES_2 = [\{A3, A4\}^{0.3}, \{A1\}^{0.6}, \Omega^{0.1}]$. Table 1 shows how these two pieces of evidence can be combined in the DS theory to further refine the context. The values in the internal boxes are the result of the combination of evidence sets $ES_1$ and $ES_2$ using Dempster's rule of combining evidence. Since by definition $m_1 \oplus m_2(\phi)$ should be equal to 0, we need to normalize the internal values in the above table by using the following general formula:

$$m_1 \oplus m_2(Z) = \left[ \sum_{Z = X \cap Y} m_1(X) \cdot m_2(Y) \right] \Big/ (1 - k) \tag{4}$$

*Table 1.*

| | $m_2[\{A1\}] = 0.6$ | $m_2[\{A3, A4\}] = 0.3$ | $m_2[(\Omega)] = 0.1$ |
|---|---|---|---|
| $m_1[\{A1, A2\}] = 0.4$ | {A1} 0.24 | $\{\phi\}$ 0.12 | {A1, A2} 0.04 |
| $m_1[\{A3\}] = 0.4$ | $\{\phi\}$ 0.24 | {A3} 0.12 | {A3} 0.04 |
| $m_1[(\Omega)] = 0.2$ | {A1} 0.12 | {A3, A4} 0.06 | $(\Omega)$ 0.02 |

where $k = \sum_{X \cap Y} = \phi\, m_1(X) \cdot m_2(Y)$. For example, in Table 1, $k = 0.12 + 0.24 = 0.36$ and $1 - k = 0.64$, the values in the boxes should be modified as follows:

$$m_1 \oplus m_2(\{\mathrm{A1}\}) = (0.24 + 0.12)/0.64 = 0.56;$$
$$m_1 \oplus m_2(\{\mathrm{A1, A2}\}) = 0.04/0.64 = 0.0625;$$
$$m_1 \oplus m_2(\{\mathrm{A3}\}) = (0.12 + 0.04)/0.64 = 0.25;$$
$$m_1 \oplus m_2(\{\mathrm{A4, A5}\}) = 0.06/0.64 = 0.093;$$
$$m_1 \oplus m_2(\Omega) = 0.02/0.64 = 0.031; \quad m_1 \oplus m_2(\phi) = 0.$$

*6.3.2.2. Why the DS approach?* The utility of probability theory for modeling reasoning with uncertainty is limited by the lack of sufficient data to accurately estimate the prior and conditional probabilities required in using Bayes' rule. The DS theory sidesteps the requirement for this data. It accepts an incomplete probabilistic model without prior or conditional probabilities. Given the incompleteness of the model, the DS theory does not answer arbitrary probabilistic questions. Rather than estimating the probability of a hypothesis, it uses belief intervals to estimate how close the evidence is to determining the truth of a hypothesis. When used to model sources of evidence that are not independent, it can yield misleading and counterintuitive results. The fact that the classification decomposes semantic conflicts into disjoint classes helps significantly in the process of avoiding errors. It is important to note that a nonmonotonic approach in accumulating assertions has provisions for retracting assertions and the DS approach can be used together with a nonmonotonic approach.

***6.3.3. The necessity of the ATMS.*** The use of the DS approach requires an inference engine to deduce belief functions. We use an ATMS to provide a symbolic mechanism for identifying the set of assumptions needed to assemble the desired proofs, so when we assign probabilities of these assumptions, the system can be used as a symbolic engine for computing degrees of belief sought by the DS theory. The second important use of the truth maintenance system is to handle the effect of retracting assumptions when they are invalidated by the evidence and to keep track of the multiple plausible sets of assertions which can coexist in the absence of complete knowledge. Truth maintenance systems arose as a way of providing the ability to do dependency backtracking when assumptions or assertions are retracted because they are contradicted by the current knowledge, and so to support nonmonotonic reasoning. Nonmonotonic reasoning is an approach in which axioms and/or rules of inference are extended to make it possible to reason with incomplete information.

## 6.4. *The SCOPES solution illustrated*

Instead of presenting the solution formally, which will only obscure the method, we opt to illustrate how SCOPES works through an example, but give sufficient detail to explicate the unfolding algorithm. In SCOPES, a context is operationally defined as a set of consistent ISCAs between schema elements from two given databases, say DB1 and DB2. The ISCAs must be consistent with respect to available, and generally incomplete, evidence. As the evidence itself may be uncertain, so is the consistency of the context. An ATMS maintains all plausible contexts as the evidence is being gathered, and rejects only those contexts that are found to be inconsistent because of certain contradictory evidence. In this way the reconciliation process takes advantage of both supportive and contradictory evidence. Let us again consider our problem of mapping query Q1 to Q2, and specifically schema elements 'SS#' from DB1 and 'ID' from DB2.

Without any knowledge about the interoperating databases, any of the $2^{12}$ subsets of assertions obtained from the set of 12 possible assertions is an equally valid context. This set of contexts forms a complete lattice under the containment relationship. Semantic reconciliation in SCOPES is the process of incrementally gathering semantic or structural evidence to refine our 'belief' or 'nonbelief' in any of $2^{12}$ contexts. A specific piece of evidence supports exactly one context. It is the greatest lower bound (glb) of all contexts that this evidence satisfies. Evidence is gathered to incrementally piece together a view of the remote schema which in turn enables us to narrow down the search space from $2^{12}$ to a manageable and tractable number and further refine the context for reconciliation. A word of caution here to the performance-minded reader: operationally, only those plausible contexts with respect to evidence are maintained. Thus the manageability is directly proportional to the amount of knowledge gathered about a remote site.

***6.4.1. The initial mappings.*** Terms in Q1 are mapped to terms in DB2 using knowledge sources such as reconciliation techniques, thesauri, concept hierarchies or ontologies. The success of the semantic reconciliation process is highly dependent on the availability of these latter sources of knowledge. The availability of an ontology-based reconciliation technique such as COIN or SemPro is advantageous since the ontology component of these approaches can be utilized in SCOPES to heuristically generate the initial correspondences between the two databases. However, the mappings obtained as a result of this exercise are not sufficient to guarantee a meaningful exchange of information among HIS. For example, in Section 3 we illustrated how the interpretations of queries Q and Q′ may be 'fixed' if we rely completely on an ontology for semantic reconciliation. Below we illustrate how SCOPES can exploit the advantages of ontologies in general while overcoming their limitations.

We asked two different DBAs to map the local schema objects from their respective databases, DB1 and DB2, to corresponding concepts in MIKROKOSMOS. Table 2 shows these mappings. Tables 3–6 show the correspondences established via MIKROKOSMOS between Ontology Concepts from DB1 and DB2. The respective similarity strength (score) given by MIKROKOSMOS for each mapping is also listed.

***6.4.2. Algorithm***

*Step 1: Initialization*

Semantic reconciliation in SCOPES is query-directed. The first step is to determine the semantic relevance of a remote database with respect to a specific information request. A

*Table 2.*

| Concepts from DB1 | Corresponding MIKROKOSMOS concepts for DB1 | Concepts from DB2 | Corresponding MIKROKOSMOS concepts for DB2 |
|---|---|---|---|
| SS# | Identify | ID | Identify |
| Faculty | University-faculty | Employee | Support-staff |
| University | University | Affiliation | Affiliate |
| Sponsor | Sponsor | Employer | Organization |
| Motorola | For-profit-organization | Consultant | Advising-entity |
| UIC | Academic-organization | Dept | Organization-division |
| Affiliation | Affiliate | Compensation | Salary-attribute |
| ... | ... | ... | ... |

*Table 3.*

| DB1 ontology concept | DB2 ontology concepts | Similarity score |
|---|---|---|
| Identify | Identify | 1.0 |
| Identify | Organization | 0.46 |
| Identify | Affiliate | 0.35 |
| Identify | Advising-entity | 0.27 |
| Identify | Support-staff | 0.24 |
| Identify | Salary-attribute | 0.118 |

*Table 4.*

| DB1 ontology concept | DB2 ontology concepts | Similarity score |
|---|---|---|
| University-faculty | Organization | 0.68 |
| University-faculty | Affiliate | 0.45 |
| University-faculty | Advising-entity | 0.40 |
| University-faculty | Support-staff | 0.40 |
| University-faculty | Identify | 0.29 |
| University-faculty | Salary-attribute | 0.13 |

*Table 5.*

| DB1 ontology concept | DB2 ontology concepts | Similarity score |
|---|---|---|
| Sponsor | Organization | 0.719 |
| Sponsor | Organization-division | 0.547 |
| Sponsor | Affiliate | 0.545 |
| Sponsor | Advising-entity | 0.422 |
| Sponsor | Support-staff | 0.30 |
| Sponsor | Identify | 0.27 |

methodology such as one proposed in [13] can be integrated within SCOPES to facilitate this process. Once the semantic relevance with respect to a query is established, for example, DB2 is selected as relevant, the semantic reconciliation process can then proceed.

*Step 2: Mapping query terms*

To find correspondences for the query terms in the remote database, the coordination algorithm in SCOPES uses the MIKROKOSMOS ontology as a heuristic. For each concept in the local database, select the correspondence with the next highest similarity not already considered or rejected. For example, the synonymy mapping between terms 'SS#'and 'ID' (i.e., between concepts 'identify' and 'identify' from Table 3) is considered first. In the absence of any further evidence, any ISCA between attributes "SS#" from DB1 and "ID" from DB2 is possible. It is reasonable to assume the synonymy relationship between these two terms to be valid. In our ATMS, this mapping will be considered as a separate context; let it be denoted as C1. SCOPES assumes C1 to be the most plausible context with respect to available evidence.

*Step 3: Schema propagation to expand exploration of context*

SCOPES pursues the validation of C1 either by *upward propagation* in the schema structure to gather evidence on the structural relationship between the entities to which the two attributes respectively belong; or by *downward propagation* in the schema structure to gather comparative evidence on the relationship between their respective domain values. Several other propagation techniques [8] are utilized to expand the exploration of the context. SCOPES can then utilize available knowledge sources such as ontology-based reconciliation techniques, to either elicit a mapping between the terms representing the entities, or to compare the domains of the two attributes. In our example, we continue using MIKROSMOS. From Table 4, this exploration via the ontology results in the following evidence: (Note again: terms 'object' and 'class' interchangeably).

E1: syn(term(Faculty, DB1), term(Employee, DB2)) with probability 0.4

Generally, evidence such as E1 may be obtained using a number of knowledge sources including ontologies, lexicons, reconciliation techniques, general or domain specific knowledge repositories, metadata specifications, general rules derived from conceptual structures etc. [18]. The strength of this evidence is determined by its source. For example, in the case above a probability of 0.4 is assigned to E1 based on the similarity score provided by MIKROKOSMOS in Table 4 for concepts (University-Faculty and Support-Staff).

*Step 4: ISCAs inference*

E1 is used below to further narrow the search space. In SCOPES the reconciliation techniques and knowledge sources are coordinated using the following interface template:

r: IF C(p) THEN consequent. $[p.q]$ (5)

where the antecedent of the rule C is defined recursively in BNF (Backus-Naur Form) as follows:

C ::= E | Assertion | Assumption | E and C | Assertion and C | Assumption and C

Additionally, C may include quantifiers over the domains of the variables. As a result, 'C' can be an extremely complex typed predicated logic expression constructed from either a directly elicited piece of evidence 'E', available knowledge, a reasonable assumption, or a combination thereof. In the above template "consequent" is a disjunction of assertions about two objects O1 and O2, $p$ represents the degree of belief in all the assertions in 'C', and $q$ is the degree of belief in rule r if $p = 1$.

There may be several rules that derive the consequent of rule r. The DS theory provides a feature called *parallel reduction* to derive the degree of belief in the consequent. However, all the matching rules need not be activated at the same time. Actually, selection of rules to activate is determined by various optimization strategies. A discussion of these strategies is beyond the scope of this paper. Let us assume the availability of the rules listed below. These rules are general, and thus independent of any specific database or application domain. (The following notation is used: Obj(O, t) denotes that Object 'O' is represented by term 't'; term(t, O) denotes that 't' is the term corresponding to object 'O'; att(t, O) denotes that term 't' represents an attribute of object 'O'; dom(O) denotes the domain of object 'O'; key(t, O) denotes that 't' is the term corresponding to the key of object 'O'.

r1: **IF** syn(t, t′) ∧ Obj(O, t) ∧ Obj(O′, t′) **THEN** syn(O, O′) ∧ (gen(O, O′) ∨ agg(O, O′) ∨ class(O, O′))

r2: **IF** syn(O, O′) ∧ att(t, O) ∧ att(t′, O′) ∧ key(t, O) ∧ key(t′, O′) **THEN** syn(t, t′)

r3: **IF** syn(O, O′) ∧ att(t, O) ∧ att(t′, O′) ∧ not(key(t, O)) ∧ not(key(t′, O′)) **THEN** syn(t, t′) ∨ hom (t, t′) ∨ nrelated(t, t′)

r4: **IF** gen(O, O′) ∧ term(t, O) ∧ term(t′, O) **THEN** gen(t, t′)

r5: **IF** dom(O) ≠ dom(O′) **THEN** hom(O, O′)

r6: **IF** $\forall v_1 \in$ dom(O), $\exists v_2 \in$ dom(O′) ∧ syn($v_1$, $v_2$) **THEN** syn(O, O′)

r7: **IF** syn (O, O′) ∧ class(O, O′) ∧ att(t, O) ∧ att(t′, O′) ∧ key(t, O) ∧ key(t′, O′) **THEN** syn(t, t′) ∧ class(t, t′)

r8: **IF** syn(O, O′) ∧ gen(O, O′) ∧ att(t, O) ∧ att(t′, O′) ∧ key(t, O) ∧ key(t′, O′) **THEN** syn(t, t′) ∧ gen(t, t′)

r9: **IF** syn(O, O′) ∧ agg(O, O′) ∧ att(t, O) ∧ att(t′, O′) ∧ key(t, O) ∧ key(t′, O′) **THEN** syn(t, t′) ∧ agg(t, t′)

The above rules clearly comply with the interface template. For simplicity, the degree of belief in each of the above rules is assumed to be $q = 1$. This is obviously an overestimation. While this may reduce the performance of the system in general because of potentially increasing backtracking during reconciliation, it avoids the perennial argument in expert systems of whether any probability assignment conforms to reality even if it is provided by experts. A rule r whose consequent is a disjunction of literals, as is rule r1, may be decomposed into as many rules as there are literals in the consequent. Each of the resulting rules will have the same premise as r and exactly one literal as consequent. The degree of belief of the original rule is then uniformly distributed over all the resulting rules.

E1 matches rule r1. The consequent leads to A1, A2 and A3.

A1: Assert[syn(Faculty, Employee), class(Faculty, Employee), obj(Faculty, DB1), obj(Employee, DB2)]
A2: Assert[syn(Faculty, Employee), gen(Faculty, Employee), obj(Faculty, DB1), obj(Employee, DB2)]
A3: Assert[syn(Faculty, Employee), agg(Faculty, Employee), obj(Faculty, DB1), obj(Employee, DB2)]

$$\text{A} = \{\text{A1}, \text{A2}, \text{A3}\}, m(\{\text{A1}, \text{A2}, \text{A3}\}) = p * q = 0.4$$

where $p = 0.4$ and $q = 1.0$, $m(\Omega) = 0.6$

Applying Eqs. (1) and (2): $Bel(A) = 0.4$ and $Pls(A) = 1$.

With a degree of belief of 0.4 we can say that A1, A2, and A3 are part of the relevant context. SCOPES can now use this belief to refine the context for ('SS#', 'ID') pair.

*Step 5: Derivation*

Evidence E2 can be deduced from the set {A1, A2, and A3}.

E2: syn(obj(Faculty, DB1), obj(Employee, DB2)) [0.4]

This is yet another example of how SCOPES gathers evidence during the reconciliation process, i.e., the consequent of rules becomes part of the body of collected evidence.

*Step 6: Repeat Steps 4 and 5 until no derivation*

Evidence E2 matches part of the premise in rule r2. The rest of the premise simply requires schema information in DB1 and DB2, which can readily be obtained with degree of belief of 1.0. The consequent of rule r2 enables us to generate the following evidence:

E2′: syn(att(SS#, Faculty, DB1), att(ID, Employee, DB2)) [0.4]

This degree of belief for E2′ is obtained by using Eq. (5). But information obtained from the ontology (see Table 3) indicates that the two attributes are synonyms with similarity score equal to 1.0. In other words, the synonymy relationship is certain. Obviously, this fact overrides any other on this matter generated by inference. This case illustrates again another situation where the availability of an ontology helps narrow the search process. The belief degree of E2′ is updated to 1.0, and thus:

A4: Assert[syn(SS#, ID), class(SS#, ID), (att(SS#, Faculty, DB1), att(ID,Employee, DB2))]
A5: Assert[syn(SS#, ID), gen(SS#, ID), (att(SS#, Faculty, DB1), att(ID, Employee, DB2))]

$$A = \{\text{A4}, \text{A5}\}, m\{\text{A4}, \text{A5}\} = 1.0 \text{ and } m(\Omega) = 0.0$$

Applying Eqs. (1) and (2) $Bel(A) = 1.0$ and $Pls(A) = 1.0$.

This is an example of **context merging**, which allows us to extrapolate consistent interpretations when combining plausible sets of assertions, derived from the mapping between two different yet schematically related pairs of objects.

*Step 7: Context merging*

If no additional evidence is available, the two contexts provided by the assertion sets {A1, A2, A3} and {A4, A5} cannot be refined further. However, since these two sets represent assertions about objects which are not entirely independent, i.e., 'SS#' is a key attribute of 'Faculty' and 'ID' is a key attribute of 'Employee', a pair-wise combination of members of these sets can be further investigated. We refer to this process as **context merging**. Context merging is a method to refine a query context by combining contexts dealing with schema related terms and eliminating those combinations that are contradictory. For example, consider the context {A1, A2, A3} for pair (Faculty, Employer) and {A4, A5} for pair {SS#, ID}. The resulting, potentially consistent, contexts are {A1, A4}, {A1, A5}, {A2, A4}, {A2, A5}, {A3, A4}, and {A3, A5}). According to rules r7, r8, and r9 in the rule base, only sets {A1, A4} and {A2, A5} are consistent since all other sets contain contradictory assertions. Figure 8 is a pictorial representation of the belief network resulting from the refinement of context discussed above.

*Step 8: Repeat Steps 2 to 7 until all query terms are processed*

SCOPES repeats the above reconciliation process for the other terms in Q1: from Table 6 the ontology yields a plausible synonymy mapping between terms 'University' in DB1 ('University' in Table 6) and 'Employer' in DB2 ('Organization' in Table 6). Again, this mapping is viewed in our ATMS as one separate context. Let this latter context be denoted C1′. Any ISCA between terms 'University' in DB1 and 'Employer' in DB2 is valid in the absence of further knowledge. Once again $2^{12}$ subsets may be considered. Heuristically, because of the high similiarity measure, SCOPES assumes C1′ as the most likely context

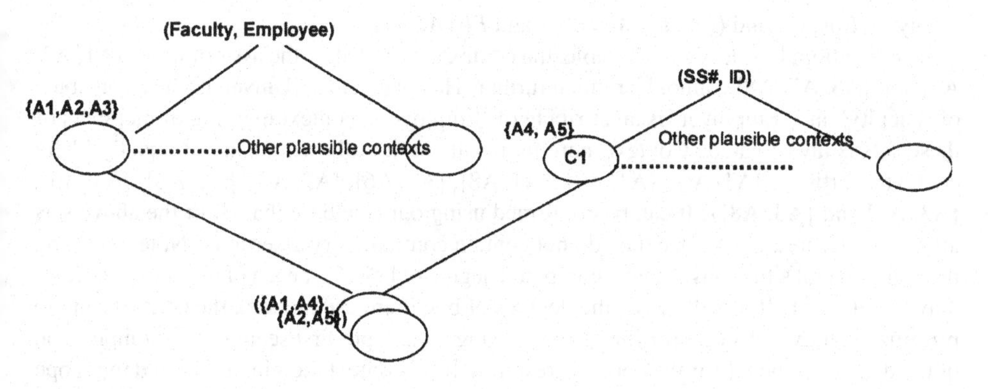


*Figure 8.*

*Table 6.*

| DB1 ontology concept | DB2 ontology concepts | Similarity score |
|---|---|---|
| University | Organization | 1.0 |
| University | Organization-division | 0.67 |
| University | Advising-entity | 0.52 |
| University | Affiliate | 0.4 |
| University | Support-staff | 0.31 |
| University | Identify | 0.25 |

and triggers further exploration through upward and downward propagation. Since the objects to which the two terms respectively belong are 'Faculty' and 'Employee', evidence E2 combined with the fact that 'University' and 'Employer' are not keys of their respective objects triggers rule r3. The consequent of rule 3 does not provide any discrimination along the naming dimension, and therefore, the search space remains potentially of size $2^{12}$ plausible contexts. In this situation, ontology knowledge is extremely useful. Knowledge from the ontology can be used as a heuristic to obtain evidence E3, which in turn triggers r1 and results in set {A6, A7, and A8}.

E3: syn(att(University, Faculty, DB1), att(Employer, Employee, DB2)) [1.0]

A6: Assert[syn(University, Employer), class(University, Employer), (att(University, Faculty, DB1), att(Employer, Employee, DB2))]
A7: Assert[syn(University, Employer), gen(University, Employer), (att(University, Faculty, DB1), att(Employer, Employee, DB2))]
A8: Assert[syn(University, Employer), agg(University, Employer), (att(University, Faculty, DB1), att(Employer, Employee, DB2))]

$$A = \{A6, A7, A8\}, m\{A6, A7, A8\} = p * q = 0.7$$
$$\text{where } p = 1.0 \text{ and } q = 0.7, m(\Omega) = 0.3$$

Applying Eqs. (1) and (2): $Bel(A) = 0.7$ and $Pls(A) = 1$.

If no additional evidence is available, the contexts provided by the assertion sets {A1, A2, A3} and {A6, A7, A8} cannot be refined further. However, since 'University' is an attribute of 'Faculty' and 'Employer' is an attribute of 'Employee', context merging of members of these sets is investigated. Context merging results in the following pairs of equally likely context assertions: {A1, A6}, {A1, A7}, {A1, A8}, {A2, A6}, {A2, A7}, {A2, A8}, {A3, A6}, {A3, A7} and {A3, A8}). It can be confirmed using our rule base that all of the above sets are valid interpretations since they do not contain contradictory assertions. Note, however, there are several situations where a computed degree of belief for each of the above contexts may be different. If it is the case, the degrees of belief are used to rank the contexts and to prioritize context selection for further processing, i.e., depth first search. The computation of the degrees of belief for the contexts resulting from context merging is beyond the scope of this paper.

*Step 7b: Generate further evidence for same terms and compute new degree of belief using DS*

SCOPES has the capability to take advantage of the query structure using available local schema information. For example, 'UIC' exists as a domain value of attribute 'University' in DB1. The latter knowledge maybe automatically elicited from a tool such as the multi-database language [8]. The coordination algorithm in SCOPES exploits this knowledge to investigate the domain of 'Employer' in DB2 to find a match for 'UIC', through downward propagation. Assume the following evidence is uncovered.

E4: dom(University) $\neq$ dom(Employer) [1.0]

The Evidence E4 matches r5 and this rule is fired. The consequent r5 enables us to conclude that the set $A$ of plausible assertions is A9.

A9: Assert[hom(University, Employer), class(University, Employer), att(University, Faculty, DB1), att(Employer, Employee, DB2))]

$$A = \{A9\}, m\{A9\} = p * q = 1.0 \quad \text{where } p = 1 \text{ and } q = 1.0, m(\Omega) = 0.0$$

Applying Eqs. (1) and (2): $Bel(A) = 0.8$ and $Pls(A) = 1$.

This is again a situation where Dempster's rule of combination can be applied to determine the combined belief resulting from evidence sets E3 and E4. This is illustrated below in Table 7.

The values in the internal boxes of Table 7 are the result of the combination of evidence sets E3 and E4. Since by definition $m_1 \oplus m_2(\phi)$ should be equal to 0, we need to normalize the internal values using Eq. (4). The values in parentheses represent the normalized values.

The assertion sets {A9} and {A6, A7, A8} are two plausible alternatives. Assertion A9 contradicts assertions A6, A7 and A8. If the belief in A9 is 1.0 then the ATMS will mark assertions A6, A7, and A8 as retracted. However, the current belief in A9 is 0.54 does not allow for the retraction of the set {A6, A7, A8} whose degree of belief is now 0.318. SCOPES chooses the one with the higher degree of belief to continue the reconciliation process, i.e., depth-first search. The set {A6, A7, A8} is temporarily retracted, until and only when reconciliation is shown impossible with the assumption of {A9}.

If no additional evidence is available, the contexts provided by the assertion sets {A1, A2, A3} and {A9} cannot be refined further. Context merging results in the following pairs:

*Table 7.*

| | $m_2[\{A9\}] = 1.0$ | $m_2[(\Omega)] = 0.0$ |
|---|---|---|
| $m_1[\{A6, A7, A8\}] = 0.4(0.318)$ | $\{\phi\}$ 0.4 | {A6, A7, A8} 0.0 |
| $m_1[(\Omega)] = 0.6(0.682)$ | {A9} 0.6 (0.54) | $(\Omega)$ 0.00 |

{A1, A9}, {A2, A9}, {A3, A9}. It can be confirmed using our rule base that all of the above sets are valid interpretations since they do not contain contradictory assertions.

Since A9 asserts a homonymy relationship between objects 'University' of DB1 and 'Employer' of DB2, it becomes necessary to find a new mapping for query term 'University' of DB1. SCOPES utilizes the next alternative mapping provided by MIKROKOSMOS in Table 6. The next two rounds of reconciliation consider successively concepts 'Department' and 'Consultant' from DB2. Each of these cases are results again in a homonymy relationship being asserted in a similar fashion as was done for concept "Employer" above. The concept 'Affiliation' of DB2 is considered next. The validation process generates the following evidence;

E5: syn(att(University, Faculty, DB1), att(affiliation, Employer, DB2)) [0.4]

A10: Assert[syn(University, Affiliation), class(University, Affiliation), (att(University, Faculty, DB1), att(Employer, Employee, DB2))]
A11: Assert[syn(University, Affiliation), gen(University, Affiliation), (att(University, Faculty, DB1), att(Employer, Employee, DB2))]
A12: Assert[syn(University, Affiliation), agg(University, Affiliation), (att(University, Faculty, DB1), att(Employer, Employee, DB2))]

We update our belief as follows:

$$A = \{\text{A10}, \text{A11}, \text{A12}\}, m\{\text{A10}, \text{A11}, \text{A12}\} = p * q = 0.4$$
$$\text{where } p = 0.4 \text{ and } q = 1.0, m(\Omega) = 0.6$$

Applying Eqs. (1) and (2): $Bel(A) = 0.4$ and $Pls(A) = 1$.

As described earlier, the coordination algorithm in SCOPES exploits the availability of any schema knowledge through upward and downward propagation; i.e., University = 'UIC', to further refine context. SCOPES will trigger reconciliation by searching domain values of 'Affiliation' to find a match for 'UIC'. Assume the following evidence is uncovered:

E6: 'UIC' $\in$ dom(University, DB1) $\wedge$ 'UIC' $\in$ dom(Affiliation, DB2) [0.6]

The Evidence E6 matches r6's premise resulting in it being fired. The consequent of r6 enables us to conclude with a confidence level of $m = 0.6$ (since $p = 0.6$ from the evidence and $q = 1.0$) the set $A$ of plausible assertions contains A10. $Bel(A) = 0.6$, $Pls(A) = 1.0$. This is again an example of a situation where Dempster's rule of combination can be applied to determine the combined belief resulting from evidence sets E5 and E6, as follows:

The values in the internal boxes of Table 8 are the result of the combination of evidence sets E5 and E6. Since by definition $m_1 \oplus m_2(\phi) = 0$, we do not need to normalize the above values. $m_1 \oplus m_2$ ({A10}) = 0.7; $m_1 \oplus m_2$ ({A10, A11, A12}) = 0.16; $m_1 \oplus m_2$ $(\Omega) = 0.24$; $m_1 \oplus m_2$ $(\phi) = 0$.

The assertion sets {A10} and {A10, A11, A12} present us with two plausible alternatives. Assertion A10 is also a member of {A10, A11, A12}. SCOPES selects the set with the higher

*Table 8.*

| | $m_2[\{A10\}] = 0.6$ | $m_2[(\Omega)] = 0.4$ |
|---|---|---|
| $m_1[\{A10, A11, A12\}] = 0.4$ | {A10} 0.24 | {A10, A11, A12} 0.16 |
| $m_1[(\Omega)] = 0.6$ | {A10} 0.36 | (Ω) 0.24 |

degree of belief, which in this case is {A10}. Once this selection is made, the set {A10, A11, A12} is no longer under consideration, however, since A10 is under consideration, only assertions A11 and A12 are marked as temporarily retracted in the ATMS.

If no additional evidence is available, the contexts provided by the assertion sets {A1, A2, A3} and {A10} cannot be refined further. Context merging results in the following pairs: {A1, A10}, {A2, A10}, {A3, A10}. It can be confirmed using our rule base that all of the above sets are valid interpretations since they do not contain contradictory assertions. The belief network in figure 9 below illustrates this context refinement process.

A process similar to one described above can establish a synonymy correspondence between 'Sponsor' in DB1 and 'Employer' in DB2. Assume that context merging in this case results in the following sets: {A1, A13}, {A2, A13}, {A3, A13} where A13 asserts that:

A13: Assert[syn(Sponsor, Employer), class(Sponsor, Employer),
(att(Sponsor, Faculty, DB1), att(Employer, Employee, DB2))]

Context merging involving all the query terms, and taking **in consideration all** the **intermediate context** merging steps such as in figure 8, results in the following two sets: {A1, A4, A10, A13} and {A2, A5, A10, A13} which are sufficient to map Q1 to Q2.

## 7. Conclusions

Shared ontologies are not a definitive solution to semantic reconciliation problems as several researchers have claimed. Through a conceptual analysis of two promising ontology-driven

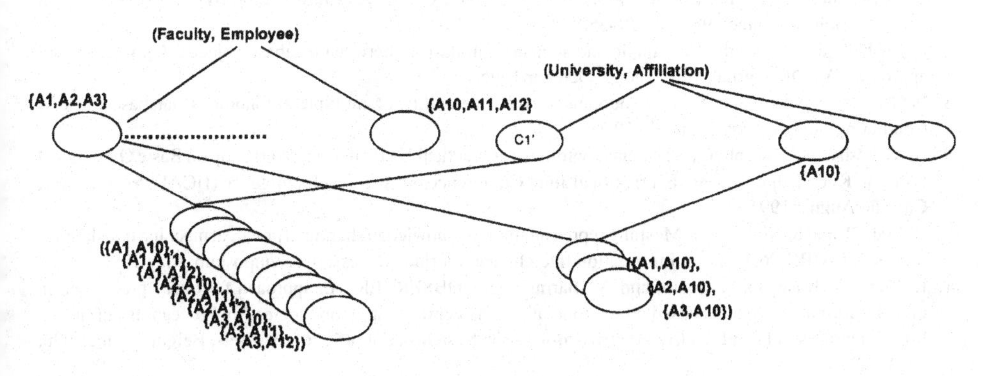


*Figure 9.*

semantic reconciliation techniques, namely COIN and SemPro, we have demonstrated their deficiencies as the sole interface between semantically heterogeneous information systems. Ontologies are useful, but they do not alone resolve semantic conflicts. We presented arguments for the set of properties needed to build truly dynamic semantic reconciliation systems. Essentially, the robustness of semantic reconciliation system rest on their capabilities to be query-directed, handle multiple interpretations in an environment of incomplete and uncertain semantic knowledge, and adapt to evolving semantics. We have described, however briefly, a system that possesses these properties, namely the SCOPES architecture, and have shown the appropriate use of a general ontology (MIKROKOSMOS). The examples demonstrated how the advantages of ontologies are exploited and their drawbacks overcome within a general coordination mechanism.

There are several issues not address here in part due to the scope of the paper. A nonexhaustive list includes: (i) performance issues, which basically deal with the pruning of the search space; other types of semantic conflicts, such as temporal, spatial and causal. An important aspect of the system is its learning capabilities. Each time a query is processed a lot of knowledge is learned by the system which may not be of direct benefit to the query at hand, but will be useful in subsequent queries assuming no significant changes occurred to the databases. We are also extending the classification to capture spatiotemporal conflicts.

## References


1. C. Batini, M. Lenzerini, and S. Navathe, "A comparative analysis of methodologies for database schema integration," ACM Computing Surveys, vol. 18, no. 4, 1986.
2. M.W. Bright, A.R. Hurson, and S. Pakzad, "Automated resolution of semantic heterogeneity in multidatabases," ACM Transactions on Database Systems, vol. 19, no. 2, pp. 212–253, June 1994.
3. J. DeKleer, "An assumption-based truth maintenance system," Artificial Intelligence, vol. 28, pp. 197–224, 1986.
4. C. Goh, M. Siegel, and S. Madnick, "Context interchange: Overcoming the challenges of large scale interoperable database systems in a dynamic environment," in Proceedings of the 3rd International Conference on Knowledge Management, Maryland, 1994, pp. 337–346.
5. T.R. Gruber, "A translation approach to portable ontology specifications," Knowledge Acquisition, vol. 5, no. 2, pp. 199–220, 1993. http://www-ksl.stanford.edu/kst/what-is-an-ontology.html
6. J. Kahng and D. McLeod, "Dynamic classificational ontologies: Mediators for sharing in cooperative federated database," in Proc. 1st IFCIS International Conference on Cooperative Information Systems (CoopIS '96), Brussels, Belgium, June 1996, pp. 26–35.
7. V. Kashyap and A. Sheth, "Schematic and semantic similarities between database objects: A context-based approach," VLDB Journal, vol. 5, no. 4, October 1996.
8. W. Litwin, I. Mark, and N. Roussoupoulos, "Interoperability of multiple autonomous databases," ACM Computing Surveys, vol. 22, no. 3, 1990.
9. K. Mahesh and S. Nirenburg, "A situated ontology for practical NLP," in Proc. Workshop on Basic Ontological Issues in Knowledge Sharing, International Joint Conference on Artificial Intelligence (IJCAI-95), Montreal, Canada, August 1995.
10. K. Mahesh and S. Nirenburg, "Meaning representation for knowledge sharing in practical machine translation," in Proc. FLAIRS-96 Track on Information Interchange, Florida AI Research Symposium, May 1996.
11. E. Mena, V. Kashyap, A. Sheth, and A. Illarramendi, "OBSERVER: An approach for query processing in global information systems based on interoperation across pre-existing ontologies," in Proceedings of the 1st IFCIS International Conf. on Cooperative Information Systems (CoopIS '96), Brussels, Belgium, June 1996, pp. 14–25.
12. MIKROKOSMOS: http://crl.nmsu.edu/Research/Projects/mikro/ontology/onto-intro-page.html

13. S. Milliner, A. Bouguettaya, and M. Papazoglou, "A scalable architecture for autonomous heterogeneous database interactions," in Proc. the 21st International Conference on Very Large Databases, VLDB '95 Proceedings, Zurich, Switzerland, September 1995.
14. C. Naiman and A. Ouksel, "A classification of semantic conflicts," Journal of Organizational Computing, vol. 5, no. 2, pp. 167–193, 1995.
15. A. Ouksel and I. Ahmed, "Plausible inference of context in heterogeneous information systems," in Proc. 5th International Workshop on Information Systems and Technology, Amsterdam, December 1995, pp. 120–129.
16. A. Ouksel and I. Ahmed, "Coordinating knowledge elicitation to support context construction in cooperative information systems," in Proc. 1st IFCIS International Conference on Cooperative Information Systems (CoopIS '96), Brussels, Belgium, June 1996, pp. 4–13.
17. A. Ouksel and I. Ahmed, "Using SCOPES for dynamic construction of context in heterogeneous information systems," in Proc. AIS 1996 Americas Conference on Information Systems, Phoenix, Arizona, August 1996, pp. 623–625.
18. A. Ouksel and C. Naiman, "Coordinating context building in heterogeneous information systems," Journal of Intelligent Information Systems, vol. 3, pp. 151–183, 1994.
19. E. Sciore, M. Siegel, and A. Rosenthal, "Using semantic values to facilitate interoperability among heterogeneous information systems," ACM Transactions on Database Systems, pp. 254–290, June 1994.
20. G. Shafer, (1976). A Mathematical Theory of Evidence, Princeton University Press, Princeton N.J.
21. A. Sheth and J. Larson, "Federated database systems," ACM Computing Surveys, vol. 22, no. 3, 1990.
22. M. Siegel and S. Madnick, "A metadata approach to resolving semantic conflicts," in Proc. 7th International Conference on Very Large Databases, September 1991, pp. 133–145.
23. G. Wiederhold, "Mediators in the architecture of future information systems," Computer, vol. 25, no. 3, March 1992.
24. L. Wittgenstein, Philosophical Investigations, Macmillan Publishing: New York, NY, 1953.
25. WWW, Refer to: Design Criteria for Ontologies: http://www.dfki.uni-kl.de/~vega/CoMem/Ontology/onto-design-gruber/ subsection3_1_2.html 28 Feb 95
26. WWW, Refer to: Plan Ontology Construction Group (POCG): KRSL 2.0.2 Ontology Hierarchy: http://isx.com/pub/ARPI/ARPI-pub/krsl/ontology-hierarchy.txt
27. C. Yu, B. Jia, W. Sun, and S. Dao, "Determining relationships among names in heterogeneous databases," SIGMOD RECORD, vol. 20, no. 4, pp. 79–80, December 1991.

Distributed and Parallel Databases, 7, 37–65 (1999)


# Controlled Vocabularies in OODBs: Modeling Issues and Implementation*

LI-MIN LIU limin@homer.njit.edu
*CIS Dept., NJIT, Newark, NJ 07102*

MICHAEL HALPER mhalper@turbo.kean.edu
*Dept. of Mathematics and Computer Science, Kean University, Union, NJ 07083*

JAMES GELLER geller@homer.njit.edu
YEHOSHUA PERL perl@homer.njit.edu
*CIS Dept., NJIT, Newark, NJ 07102*

*Received March 24, 1998; Accepted June 10, 1998*

**Recommended by:** Athman Bouguettaya

**Abstract.** A major problem that arises in many large application domains is the discrepancy among terminologies of different information systems. The terms used by the information systems of one organization may not agree with the terms used by another organization even when they are in the same domain. Such a situation clearly impedes communication and the sharing of information, and decreases the efficiency of doing business. Problems of this nature can be overcome using a controlled vocabulary (CV), a system of concepts that consolidates and unifies the terminologies of a domain. However, CVs are large and complex and difficult to comprehend. This paper presents a methodology for representing a semantic network-based CV as an object-oriented database (OODB). We call such a representation an Object-Oriented Vocabulary Repository (OOVR). The methodology is based on a structural analysis and partitioning of the source CV. The representation of a CV as an OOVR offers both the level of support typical of database management systems and an abstract view which promotes comprehension of the CV's structure and content. After discussing the theoretical aspects of the methodology, we apply it to the MED and InterMED, two existing CVs from the medical field. A program, called the OOVR Generator, for automatically carrying out our methodology is described. Both the MED-OOVR and the InterMED-OOVR have been created using the OOVR Generator, and each exists on top of ONTOS, a commercial OODBMS. The OOVR derived from the InterMED is presently available on the Web.

**Keywords:** Controlled Vocabulary, Object-Oriented Database, Object-Oriented Modeling, Terminology, Ontology, Ontology Modeling

## 1. Introduction

As the norm, different enterprises, whether they be in healthcare, manufacturing, financial services, or some other business, employ their own *ad hoc* terminologies that hinder communication and sharing of information. In the healthcare field, cases have been reported of differences between the terminologies used by different laboratories within the same hospital [7]! Such industries and areas of commerce need controlled vocabularies

* This research was (partially) done under a cooperative agreement between the National Institute of Standards and Technology Advanced Technology Program (under the HIIT contract #70NANB5H1011) and the Healthcare Open Systems and Trials, Inc. consortium.

(CVs)—systems of concepts that consolidate and unify the terminology of large application domains [9]. By maintaining a common, centralized CV, costly and time-consuming translation tasks can be eliminated from the lines of communication existing between different organizations and between the information systems each employs. A CV can also help standardize common information processing chores and thus reduce the overall cost of doing business.

The semantic network [27, 48] has proven to be an excellent modeling tool for CVs [8, 9]. However, in the face of a very large CV—encountered in many domains—a potential user or application developer might shy away from employing it due to the overwhelming complexity. It is well known that the components of the human cognitive apparatus have numeric limitations. For instance, it is accepted that human short-term memory is limited to "seven plus or minus two" chunks [32]. In a similar vein, there are well known limitations of the visual system [3]. Semantic networks and database design methodologies (like the ER model [6]) are popular because of their graphical representations, among other reasons. According to common experience, a graphical network display with around twenty concepts appears to be within human cognitive limitations, while for a graphical structure with thousands or tens of thousands of concepts, this is certainly not the case.

The reliance on a semantic network model for CVs can also be problematic from a practical standpoint. Although many useful semantic network processing systems exist (see, e.g., [2, 31, 45]), for unclear reasons, semantic networks have never taken off as commercial products. Because of this, technical support, multi-user access, documentation, and even adequate editing tools are often not available. This makes the use of a CV implemented as a semantic network a risky proposition for application developers whose environments often need exactly these missing features.

In this paper, we address these problems by introducing a methodology for representing a semantic network-based CV as an object-oriented database (OODB) [25, 54], a representation we call an Object-Oriented Vocabulary Repository (OOVR, pronounced "over"). Our methodology is based on a structural analysis and partitioning of the source CV. The schema yielded by this process is an important new layer of abstraction on top of the semantic network. The schema may, in fact, be several orders of magnitude smaller than the actual content of a large CV. Its size is more in line with the limitations of the human cognitive system than the potentially overwhelming concept network. A schema that correctly abstracts the major features of the network structures will be effective as a vehicle for exploring, studying, and ultimately comprehending the CV's subject-matter. As stated by James Cimino, the principal designer of an extensive medical CV called the Medical Entities Dictionary (MED): "The schema highlights the essence of the vocabulary while hiding minutiae" [7]. Indeed, in [16], we showed how the schematic representation of the MED helped its designers readily uncover and correct several inconsistencies and errors in the MED's original modeling. We have built an *analogical*, Web-based interface that exploits the two different view levels offered by the OODB representation (i.e., the schema-level view and the concept-level view) to facilitate interactive access to a CV [18]. By providing access to both the original CV and the schema layer, the interface allows a user to choose a verbose or compact representation for the display of the vocabulary knowledge.

Of course, utilizing an OODB also allows us to leverage all the features offered by top-of-the-line OODB management systems, which are commercially available (see, e.g.,

[14, 39, 41, 44, 52]). In its OOVR form, the CV can be accessed declaratively using the OQL standard [5] and other SQL extensions like ONTOS's OSQL [42], or using a "path" language such as XQL [24]. The OOVR also offers a "low impedance" pathway [54] to the CV's knowledge for application programs like intelligent information-locators, decision-support systems, and end-user browsers which are being built using object-oriented programming languages and technology. Concepts represented as objects in the OOVR are represented the same way within those applications. Therefore, the movement of and access to the concepts is greatly facilitated.

We have built a program called the *OOVR Generator* which automatically carries out all phases of our methodology. It takes as its input a CV in a "flat" semantic-network format and produces an equivalent, fully populated OOVR as its output. Both the formal aspects of the methodology and the details of this accompanying software will be described.

In order to demonstrate our methodology, we will be applying it to two existing CVs, the MED and the InterMED, both from the medical domain. The MED is a large CV containing about 48,000 concepts. It was developed and is currently in use at Columbia-Presbyterian Medical Center (CPMC) [8]. The InterMED was created as an offshoot of the MED [40, 46] for a more general healthcare setting. It comprises about 2,500 concepts. The representations of these two CVs as OODBs will be called the MED-OOVR and the InterMED-OOVR, respectively. Both are currently up and running on top of the ONTOS DB/Explorer, a commercial OODB management system [41, 42, 47]. The InterMED-OOVR is accessible via the Web [43] using the browser described in [18].

Even though both of the demonstration CVs are from the medical field, the methodology is applicable to CVs from any application domain. All we assume is that the vocabulary is—or can be—represented as a semantic network [53] of concepts containing a concept-subsumption (IS-A) hierarchy. We will discuss more of the details of the assumed representation in the next section.

The remainder of this paper is organized as follows. In Section 2, we present background material, including an overview of the general structure of CVs that are amenable to our methodology (including the MED and InterMED), and a discussion of related research work. Section 3 presents the details of the OODB representation of the CV. Software which automatically creates and populates an OOVR with respect to a given CV is presented in Section 4. Section 5 contains the conclusions.

## 2. Background

### 2.1. *Structural Form of a CV*

A common formalism used in the construction of CVs, including both the MED and the InterMED, is the semantic network [27, 53]. A CV is a collection of nodes, each of which represents a single concept. A concept can have two kinds of properties, attributes and relationships. An attribute is a property whose value is from some data type (such as an integer or text string). A relationship, on the other hand, has as its value a reference to another concept in the CV. Each concept has a unique name which is often called its *term* [13]. A term is stored as the attribute *name* of its concept. An example of a relationship found in the MED, as well as in the InterMED, is *part-of* which links a source concept to the concept of which it is definitionally a part.

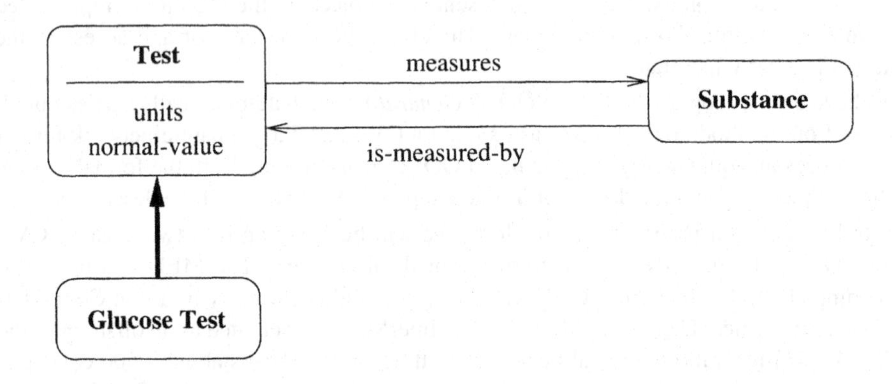


*Figure 1.* Concepts **Test**, **Substance**, and **Glucose Test**

We will be using the following graphical conventions when drawing the elements of a CV. A concept is a rectangle having rounded edges with its name (term) written inside. The names of any attributes introduced by the concept (when shown) are written below the concept's name and are separated from it by a line. Note that the values of such attributes will not be included in any diagrams. A relationship is a labeled arrow directed from the source concept to the target concept. As an example, we show the concepts **Test**[1] and **Substance** in Figure 1. The concept **Test** introduces the two attributes *units* and *normal-value* and the relationship *measures* directed to **Substance**. The concept **Substance** introduces the relationship *is-measured-by* (the converse of *measures*) but no attributes.

Following [8, 9], CVs are assumed to adhere to the design criteria of *nonredundancy* and *synonymy*, among others. The nonredundancy criterion states that a concept must be represented by a single node in the network. Of course, a concept may be known by several names. This is addressed by the synonymy criterion which states that the CV should maintain these alternative names (i.e., synonyms) with the single node. To accommodate this, all concepts have the attribute *synonyms*. Thus, a concept's primary designation (i.e., its term) is stored in the attribute *name*, while any secondary designations (i.e., its synonyms) are stored in the attribute *synonyms*. Determining which name is primary and which are secondary is strictly a design decision. The point is that all acceptable names are stored directly with the concept, and the concept is accessible via any of them.

An important feature of a CV is the concept-subsumption hierarchy, a singly-rooted, directed acyclic graph (DAG) of concepts connected via IS-A links. This hierarchy serves two main purposes. First, it supports the inheritance of properties among concepts within the CV. A subconcept is defined to inherit all the properties of its superconcept(s). For example, **Glucose Test** IS-A **Test** and therefore inherits all of **Test**'s properties. In other words, the set of properties of **Glucose Test** is a superset of the properties of **Test**. An IS-A link is drawn as a bold, unlabeled arrow directed from the subconcept to the superconcept as shown in Figure 1. Because the IS-A hierarchy is a DAG, a concept may have more than one superconcept (or parent). In such a case, the subconcept inherits from all its parents. As we will discuss further below, most CVs exhibit what we call *sparse inheritance* which influenced our design decisions.

The second purpose of the hierarchy is to support reasoning in the form of subsumption-based inferences. For example, using the fact that **Tetracycline** IS-A **Antibiotic**, a decision-support system can infer that a patient is on antibiotics from an entry in a clinical database stating that the patient is taking tetracycline.

As noted, the IS-A hierarchy is singly-rooted. We refer to the root concept as **Entity**. Note that this requirement does not affect generality because such a concept can be artificially introduced, if necessary.

We will be using the MED and the InterMED as source vocabularies to demonstrate our methodology. The MED comprises about 48,000 concepts which are connected by more than 61,000 IS-A links and 71,000 non-hierarchical (i.e., non-IS-A) relationships. The figures for the InterMED are as follows: approximately 2,500 concepts, 3,400 IS-A links, and 3,500 non-hierarchical relationships.

Both the MED and InterMED obey the following rule pertaining to the introduction of properties into the vocabulary.

**Rule (Uniqueness of Property Introduction):** A given property $x$ can be introduced at only one concept in the CV.

If other concepts also need $x$, then they must be defined as descendants of the concept at which $x$ is introduced and obtain it by inheritance. We will be assuming that any CV to which our methodology is to be applied satisfies the above rule. Note that this is not overly restrictive because if there is a need to introduce a property $x$ at several independent concepts, then an "artificial" superconcept of these can be created for the purpose of defining $x$ [7].

### 2.2. *Related Research Work*

Computerizing natural language concepts has long been a major goal of computer scientists. Various forms of semantic networks [2, 27, 48, 53], knowledge representation languages [23, 31, 35], ontologies [38], and semantic data models [19, 20] have been recruited to tackle this task. While most attempts have been limited to small domains or "toy" applications, there have been a number of notable exceptions such as CYC [29] and WordNet [33].

Aside from the MED and the InterMED, the medical field has seen the introduction of a number of CVs. These include UMLS [49], SNOMED [10], and ICD9-CM [50]. A descriptive semantic network called Structured Meta Knowledge (SMK), employing a terminological knowledge-base, has been used to capture the semantics of patients' medical records [15].

An object-oriented framework has previously been employed as a modeling platform for thesauri used in (natural) language-to-language translation [12, 13]. TEDI, a terminology editor, was built in the same context as a tool for extracting relevant information from hypermedia documents [34]. The $O_2$ OODB system [11, 47] has been used to store portions of a general English dictionary based on a "feature structure" description of its entries [21]. In a similar effort, [55] presents a technique for storing a dictionary in an ObjectStore database [26, 47].

Database technology has been used as a means for bringing persistence to knowledge-based systems. In [22], the EXODUS object manager [4] is used as a subsystem of a frame representation system [23]. A storage model, based on techniques previously proposed for OODBs [51], has been employed as the basis for storing Telos knowledge-bases on disk [36]. Both these efforts sought to incorporate their database subsystems transparently. In contrast, we are directly utilizing a commercial OODB system for the representation of our CV. After the conversion of the CV into the form of an OODB, the original semantic network version of the CV is no longer needed. Users of the vocabulary, whether they be programmers or casual browsers, can directly access the vocabulary through the various mechanisms provided by the OODB management system.

A preliminary version of our methodology appeared previously in [30]. In that paper, we applied it to the InterMED. In this paper, a substantially cleaner way of capturing our methodology is presented, and some gaps in the original treatment in [30] are filled in. We also show the application of the methodology to the much larger MED. In addition, we describe the algorithms which automatically carry out the conversion of a CV into its OOVR representation.

## 3. Representing a CV as an OODB

In this section, we present our methodology for representing a CV as an OODB. The methodology attacks this modeling problem by extracting a schematic representation from the source CV and then assigning the CV's concepts to appropriate object classes. In the source CV, there are concepts; in the OOVR, there will be objects which denote those concepts. Our methodology derives a schema with far fewer classes than the number of concepts in the source CV. The tasks are to determine how many classes are necessary, what the classes will look like, what their relationships will be, and to which classes the various concepts will belong.

In the following, we first present the version of our methodology which is applicable to CVs that do not contain *intersection concepts*, a notion which will be further discussed and formally defined below. The extended methodology that encompasses CVs exhibiting intersection concepts is described in Section 3.2.

### *3.1. OODB Schema for CVs without Intersection Concepts*

The OODB schema produced by our approach is derived automatically from an overall structural analysis of the CV. It is based on the partitioning of the CV into groups of concepts that exhibit the exact same set of properties. To be more precise, we will need the following definition, where we use $P(x)$ to denote the entire set of properties of the concept $x$.

**Definition 1 (Area):** Let $A$ be a non-empty set of concepts such that $\forall x, y \in A, P(x) = P(y)$. For such a set, let $P(A) = P(x)$ for some $x \in A$. That is, $P(A)$ is the set of properties exhibited by each of $A$'s members. $A$ is called an *area* if there does not exist a set of concepts $B$ such that $\forall v, w \in B, P(v) = P(w)$, $P(B) = P(A)$, and $A \subset B$. In other words, $A$ is an area if it is the maximal set of concepts which exhibit the set of properties $P(A)$. □

By definition, if $A_1$ and $A_2$ are areas, and $A_1 \neq A_2$, then $A_1 \cap A_2 = \emptyset$. That is, distinct areas are always disjoint. Given this fact, it is relatively straightforward to define the OODB schema of a CV if one knows all the CV's areas. For each area $A$, a class having the properties $P(A)$ is created. While this description leaves out some important details, it does capture the essence of the approach. The problem, of course, lies in the identification of the areas.

In the remainder of this section, we will be describing the process of identifying all areas in the CV—and, hence, partitioning the CV into mutually exclusive sets—under the assumption that the CV does not contain *intersection concepts*, which will be formally defined in the next subsection. (Informally, an intersection concept is one that does not introduce any new properties but still has a different set of properties from all its parents due to inheritance from several of them.) After discussing the area-partitioning, we will present the details of the OODB schema derived directly from it and describe how the CV is stored in the database.

The methodology as presented in this section is sufficient in itself for a CV whose IS-A hierarchy is a tree. Examples of such CVs include ICD-9 [50] and AHFS [1]. Even if the hierarchy is a DAG, the methodology will still be suitable if the CV is devoid of intersection concepts, a condition that can be detected algorithmically. An example of such a CV is NDC [37]. The main reason for delaying consideration of intersection concepts to the next section is that it greatly simplifies the presentation.

The identification of areas follows the pattern in which the concepts' properties are introduced into the CV. In this regard, we will need the following two definitions. In the first, we use $\Pi(x)$ to denote the set of properties intrinsically introduced or defined by the concept $x$ (as opposed to those that are inherited by it).

**Definition 2 (Property-Introducing Concept):** A concept $x$ is called a property-introducing concept if $\Pi(x) \neq \emptyset$, i.e., if it intrinsically defines one or more properties. □

**Definition 3 (Direct Property-Introducing Descendant [DPID]):** Let $v$ and $w$ be property-introducing concepts, and let $w$ be a descendant of $v$ with respect to the IS-A hierarchy. The concept $w$ is called a direct property-introducing descendant (DPID) of $v$ if there exists an upwardly directed IS-A path (there can be more than one) from $w$ to $v$ that does not contain another property-introducing concept. □

The property-introducing concepts form the basis for the areas of the CV. In fact, in a CV devoid of intersection concepts, we can equivalently state the definition of area in terms of property-introducing concept as follows:

**Definition 4 (Area [equivalent redefinition]):** An area is a set of concepts containing a property-introducing concept $v$ and all of $v$'s descendants excluding its DPIDs and their respective descendants. □

Clearly, an area can contain only a single property-introducing concept. Any descendants that are also property-introducing concepts will define new areas of their own. From a top-down vantage point, the property-introducing concept is the highest node in an area, and in this sense it "starts" the area. For this reason, we refer to that concept as the *root* of the area and use it when we need to assign a name to the area.

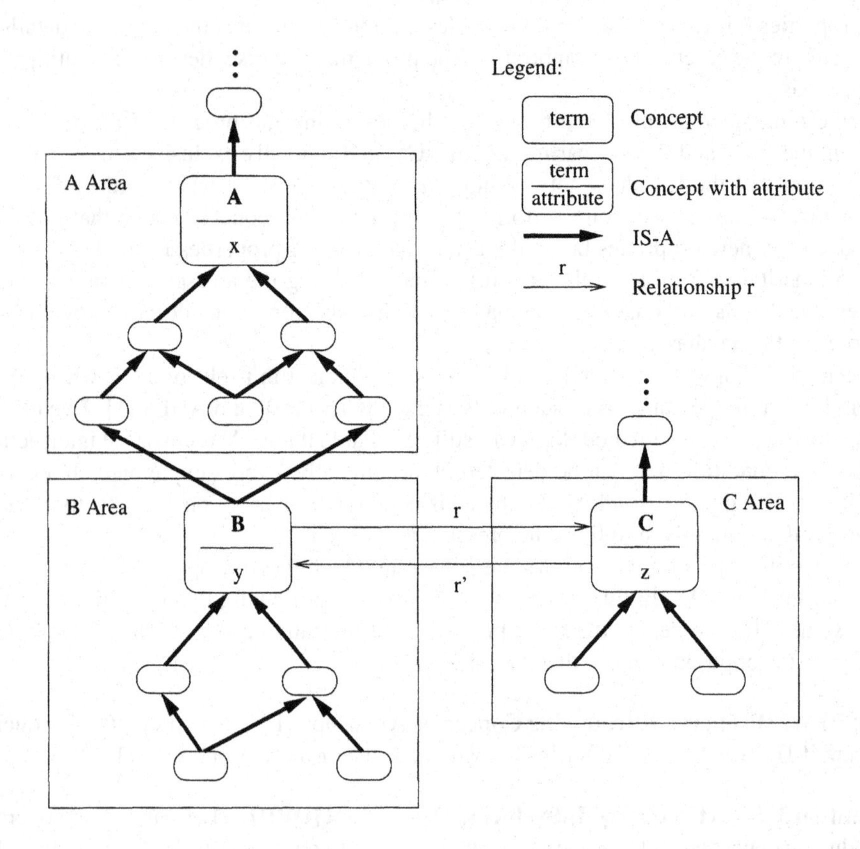


*Figure 2.* Three areas of a CV

To illustrate the partitioning of a CV, we show three areas $A$, $B$, and $C$ in Figure 2. The concepts are drawn as rectangles with rounded edges, while the areas are shown as large rectangles. Note that the root of area $A$ (i.e., the concept **A**) introduces the single attribute $x$. Area $A$ extends down to, but excludes, node **B** which is a DPID of **A**. **B** defines the attribute $y$ as well as the relationship $r$ and serves as the root of area $B$. Finally, area $C$ has the root **C** which introduces attribute $z$ and the relationship $r'$, the converse of $r$. The ellipses in the figure indicate the omission of additional concepts above the areas $A$ and $C$.

As concrete examples, we show portions of three areas from the MED in Figure 3. The concept **Event Component** introduces the new attribute *event-component-display-name*

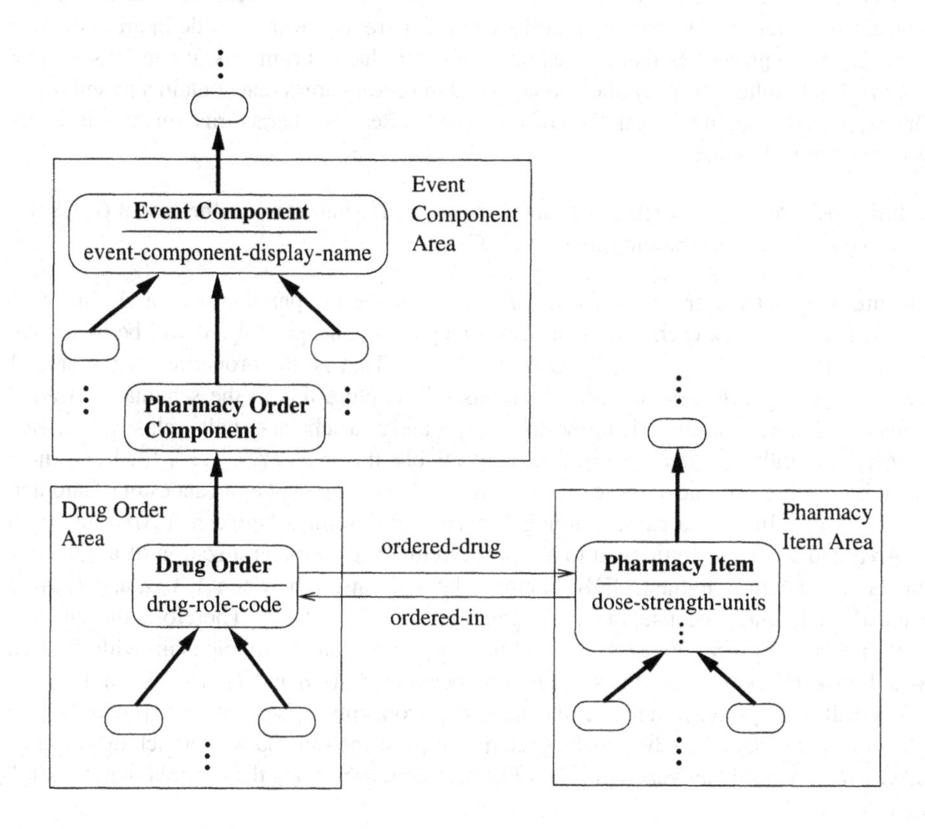


*Figure 3.* Three areas from the MED

and is thus the root of a new area, "Event Component" area. The concept **Pharmacy Order Component** also resides in that area. **Drug Order** introduces two properties: the attribute *drug-role-code*, and the relationship *ordered-drug* pointing at **Pharmacy Item**. **Drug Order** therefore roots the "Drug Order" area. Finally, **Pharmacy Item** defines the attribute *dose-strength-units* (among others) and the relationship *ordered-in*, and serves as the root of "Pharmacy Item" area.

Another example is the area rooted at the concept **Entity**, which, as we noted above, is assumed to be the top concept of all CVs. **Entity** introduces a number of properties (including *name*) and is therefore the root of "Entity" area.

Once all the areas of the CV have been identified, the OODB schema can be created as follows. For each area $A$, define a class (called *A_Area*) whose instances will be exactly the concepts in $A$, including $A$'s root (call it $r_A$). As all concepts in $A$ possess the same set of properties as $r_A$ [namely, $P(r_A)$], it seems natural to define the properties of *A_Area* to be $P(r_A)$. However, this ignores the fact that $r_A$ may have inherited some of its properties rather than defined them all intrinsically. In fact, it is only necessary to endow *A_Area* with the set of intrinsic properties of $r_A$, $\Pi(r_A)$. The rest of the properties can be obtained via OO subclass inheritance. The root $r_A$ inherits from its parents—which reside in areas distinct from $A$—those properties that it does not itself introduce. From this, it can be seen that *A_Area* should inherit from all the classes which represent areas that contain a parent of $r_A$. That is, *A_Area* should be a subclass of all those classes. To characterize this precisely, let us define the following.

**Definition 5 (Parent [Area]):** Let $B$ and $C$ be areas. If a parent of $r_C$, the root of $C$, resides in $B$, then $B$ is called a parent (area) of $C$. □

Continuing, let the areas $T_1, T_2, \ldots, T_n$ $(n \geq 1)$ be the parents of area $A$. In other words, $T_1, T_2, \ldots, T_n$ each contain at least one parent concept of $r_A$. It will be noted that $P(A) = \Pi(r_A) \cup P(T_1) \cup P(T_2) \cup \cdots \cup P(T_n)$. That is, the properties of the area $A$ are gathered from its root and all its parents. To capture this in the schema, *A_Area* is defined with the set of intrinsic properties $\Pi(r_A)$, and as a subclass of all $n$ classes $T_1$*_Area*, $T_2$*_Area*, through $T_n$*_Area* representing, respectively, the areas $T_1, T_2, \ldots, T_n$. Let us note that it is possible that one of these classes, say, $T_i$*_Area* is a parent or an ancestor of another, say, $T_j$*_Area*. In such a case, defining subclass relationships between *A_Area* and both $T_i$*_Area* and $T_j$*_Area* would lead to a "short circuit" (i.e., a materialization of a transitive subclass connection) in the OODB schema. The relationship between *A_Area* and $T_i$*_Area* is clearly redundant because, in such a situation, $P(T_i) \subset P(T_j)$. Therefore, the subclass relationship to $T_j$*_Area* gives *A_Area* all the properties that the relationship with $T_i$*_Area* would provide. Due to this, the subclass link between *A_Area* and $T_i$*_Area* is omitted.

Since all concepts (except for **Entity**) have superconcepts, $r_A$'s parents will probably have their own parents, and so the subclass relationships of the schema will branch upward in a DAG structure until they reach the class *Entity_Area* representing the top area (i.e., "Entity" area) of the CV.

In Figure 4, we show the three classes that represent the areas from Figure 2. A class is drawn as a rectangle; its intrinsic attributes are listed inside beneath its name. A subclass relationship is denoted as a bold arrow directed upward from the subclass to its superclass, and a relationship is represented by a labeled thin arrow. As we see, *A_Area* has the attribute $x$ defined by the concept **A**, the root of the area. Likewise, *B_Area* has the attribute $y$ and the relationship $r$, and *C_Area* has the attribute $z$ and the relationship $r'$. Note that *B_Area* is a subclass of *A_Area* because area $A$ contains the parents of concept **B**, the root of area $B$.

Referring back to the sample areas from the MED in Figure 3, "Event Component" area would have the corresponding class *Event_Component_Area*, which defines the attribute *event-component-display-name*. The "Drug Order" area would have the class *Drug_Order_-Area* with the attribute *drug-role-code* and the relationship *ordered-drug*. The class *Pharmacy_Item_Area* with the appropriate properties would denote the "Pharmacy Item" area. Lastly, "Entity" area would be associated with the class *Entity_Area* possessing the property *name* and so forth. It should be noted that *Entity_Area* is the root class of the schema.

One final aspect of the OODB that warrants special consideration is the representation of the CV's IS-A hierarchy. We have already used this feature and, more specifically, its inheritance mechanism to derive the subclass relationships of the schema. However, it is

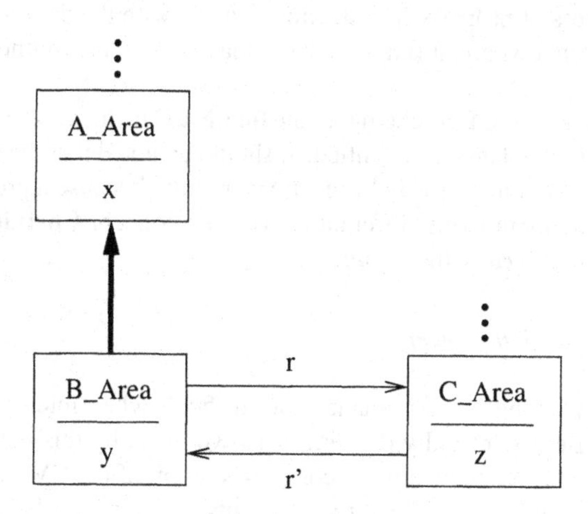


*Figure 4.* Area classes corresponding to the three areas in Figure 2

still required that the individual concepts themselves (at the instance-level of the OODB) be connected to their parents (and vice versa). This can be done by once again noting that all concepts in the CV, except for the root, have parents. Thus, we equip all concepts with two additional generic relationships, "has-superconcept" and "has-subconcept," which connect a concept to its parents and children, respectively. Within the semantic network, these relationships can be seen as being defined by **Entity** and inherited by every other concept. Following that, they are defined reflexively at the root class *Entity_Area* of the OODB schema. If, in the original CV, concept $x$ IS-A $y$, then, in the OODB, the object representing $y$ is a referent of $x$ with respect to the *has_superconcept* relationship; conversely, $x$ is a referent of $y$ via *has_subconcept*.

Because the direct extension of a class in the OODB schema is precisely one area, we refer to it as an *area class*. Overall, the schema comprises a collection of area classes. Since it is an abstraction of the property definitions and accompanying inheritance that occur within a CV as modeled by a semantic network, we call this kind of schema a *network abstraction schema*.

It is important to point out that the area-partitioning described above does not lead to a proliferation of classes in the OODB schema. There are two major reasons for this: (a) typically, there is a small number of distinct properties in a CV compared to the total number of concepts; and (b) the "uniqueness of property introduction" rule. Due to the latter, one does not find redundant property introductions strewn throughout the CV. Since property-introducing concepts always start new areas, this helps keep their numbers down.

Point (a) is, fortunately, a general characteristic of CVs which stems from the fact that they are definitional structures rather than dynamic data stores. In the InterMED, there are only 51 distinct properties for a total of about 2,500 concepts. For the MED, the number is 150 properties for approximately 48,000 concepts. As a consequence of this, very few concepts intrinsically introduce properties; most properties are inherited. There are just 26 property-introducing concepts in the InterMED and 57 in the MED. It is interesting to contrast this sparseness of property introduction in a CV with the denseness of the same in a typical OODB schema where at (almost) every class we expect to find the definitions of new properties.

In Figure 5, we show the OODB schema for the InterMED in the case where its intersection concepts (and their descendants) are omitted. It should be noted that the subclass hierarchy of such a schema does not necessarily have a tree structure because a property-introducing concept can have parents in many different areas. The concept **Chemical** is an example. See the class *Chemical_Area* in the figure.

### 3.2. *CVs with Intersection Concepts*

The problem of identifying areas is made more difficult when intersection concepts are present in the CV. Before formally defining what we mean by this notion, let us give an illustration. In Figure 6, we show a more complex version of the CV excerpt appearing in Figure 2. In the following, we will call two concepts *ancestrally related* if there exists an ancestor/descendant relationship between them.

According to our specification of an area in terms of a property-introducing concept given in the previous section, the concepts **D**, **E**, **F**, and **G** (enclosed in a large box) should belong to the area rooted at **B** (i.e., area $B$) since they are "between" it and one of its DPIDs, namely, **H**. However, on closer inspection, they similarly belong to the area $C$. On the other hand, those concepts cannot belong to area $B$ (area $C$) since they have extra properties not in $P(B)$ ($P(C)$) which they inherit from $C$ ($B$). In fact, they make up a new area of their own, even though none is a property-introducing concept. They obtain their properties via inheritance from two other areas that are, in a sense, independent. Each of the concepts **D** and **E** can be seen to lie at the juncture of some inheritance paths emanating downward from the ancestrally unrelated property-introducing concepts **B** and **C**. For this reason, we call **D** and **E** *intersection concepts*. While we could formalize this notion in terms of IS-A paths, it is simpler to do it as follows.

**Definition 6 (Intersection Concept):** Let $x$ be a concept which is not a property-introducing concept and which has multiple superconcepts $t_1, t_2, \ldots, t_n$ ($n > 1$). Then $x$ is called an intersection concept if it satisfies the following: $\forall i\colon 1 \leq i \leq n$, $P(x) \neq P(t_i)$. In other words, the set of properties of $x$ differs from the set of properties of each of $x$'s parents. □

Note that a concept having a single parent cannot be an intersection concept: Its properties could only differ from its parent's if it intrinsically introduced some, in which case it would be a property-introducing concept. Furthermore, at least two of an intersection concept's parents must be from different areas. Another characteristic of intersection concepts, which has bearing on the area-partitioning of the CV, is that two such concepts having identical sets of properties (e.g., **D** and **E**) cannot be ancestrally related.

For CVs containing intersection concepts—e.g., the MED and the InterMED—there are two different kinds of areas. The first, discussed in the previous subsection, starts at a single property-introducing concept and extends downward until other property-introducing concepts or intersection concepts are reached. The second kind, defined below, is rooted

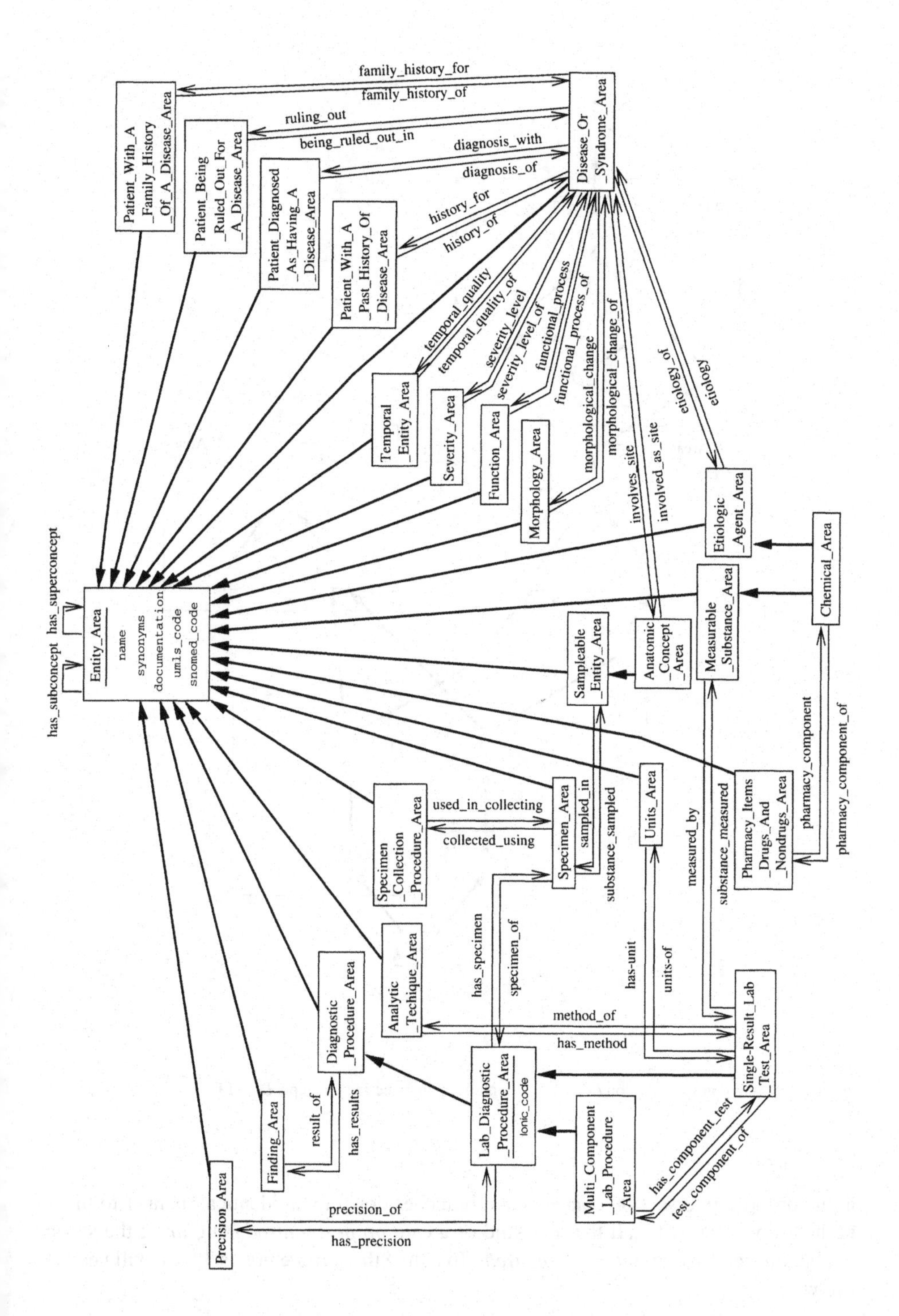


*Figure 5.* Schema for the InterMED excluding intersection concepts

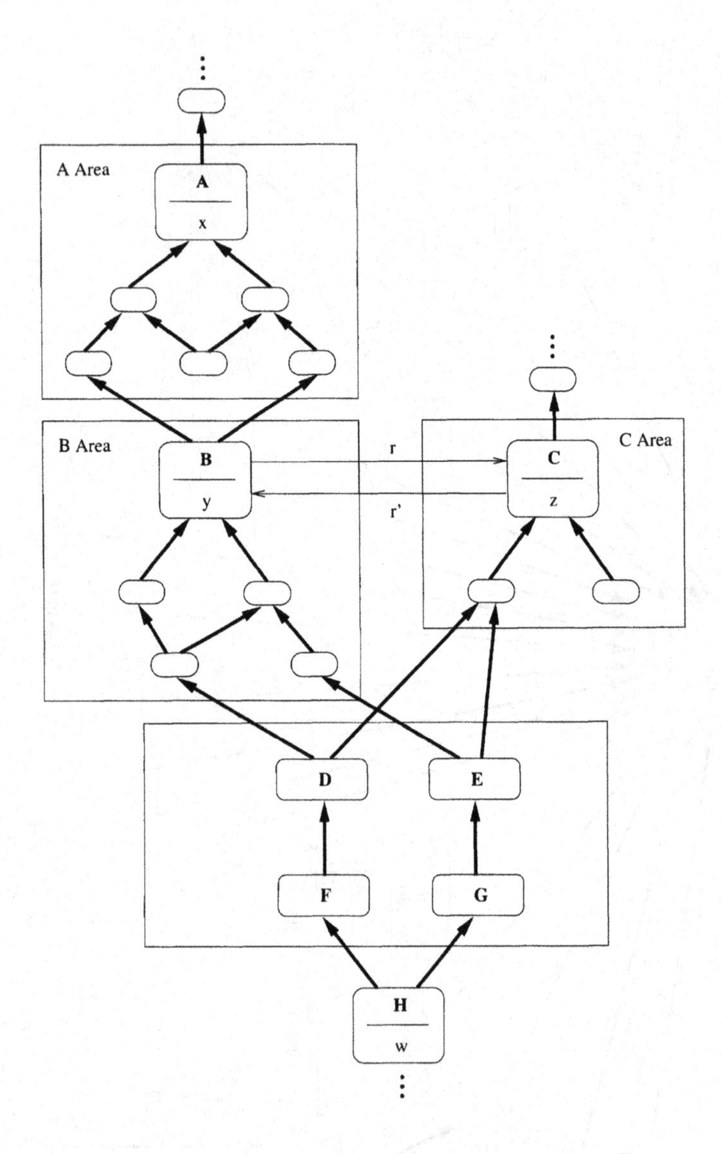


*Figure 6.* A more complex version of Figure 2 containing intersection concepts **D** and **E**

in one or more intersection concepts and branches down in an identical manner to that of the first kind. We will call the first kind of area a *property-introducing area*; the second will be referred to as an *intersection area*. To define these more precisely, we will need the following.

**Definition 7 (Direct Intersection Descendant [DID]):** Let $v$ be a property-introducing concept, $w$ be an intersection concept, and let $w$ be a descendant of $v$ with respect to the IS-A hierarchy. The concept $w$ is called a direct intersection descendant (DID) of $v$ if there exists an upwardly directed IS-A path (there can be more than one) from $w$ to $v$ that does not contain another property-introducing concept or intersection concept. □

In Definitions 3 and 7, we use a property-introducing concept $v$ as the ancestor with respect to which DPID and DID are defined. It is a straightforward matter to define both DPID and DID with respect to an intersection concept ancestor, as well. We omit these two additional definitions for the sake of brevity. We will, however, be utilizing them and referring to an intersection concept's DPIDs and DIDs below.

**Definition 8 (Property-introducing Area):** A property-introducing area is a set of concepts containing a property-introducing concept $v$ and all of $v$'s descendants excluding its DPIDs and DIDs and their respective descendants. □

**Definition 9 (Intersection Area):** Let $E = \{e_1, e_2, \ldots, e_n\}$ be a set of intersection concepts (as defined in Definition 6) such that $\forall i, j : 1 \leq i, j \leq n$, $P(e_i) = P(e_j)$. Furthermore, let $E$ be maximal, i.e., there does not exist an intersection concept $s \notin E$ such that $P(s) = P(e_k)$ for some $k$. Now, $\forall i : 1 \leq i \leq n$, let $E_i$ be the set containing $e_i$ and all of $e_i$'s descendants excluding its DPIDs and DIDs and their respective descendants. The set $I = E_1 \cup E_2 \cup \cdots \cup E_n$ is called an intersection area. □

The concepts $e_1, e_2, \ldots, e_n$ will be called the roots of the intersection area because each starts a portion of it. These portions may overlap. The name of the area can be chosen arbitrarily (perhaps by the vocabulary administrator) from among the $n$ concepts.

Referring back to Figure 6, we see that the four concepts, **D**, **E**, **F**, and **G**, constitute an intersection area. Both **D** and **E** are intersection concepts and serve as the roots of the area. The concepts **F** and **G** are not roots. Indeed, they are not intersection concepts but happen to reside in an intersection area by dint of their IS-A connections to intersection concepts.

In the InterMED, only 2 of its 2,500 concepts are intersection concepts. For the MED, it is 1,332 out of 48,000. An example of an intersection concept in the InterMED is **Water** whose parents reside in two areas: "Sampleable Entity" area and "Chemical" area. An intersection concept from the MED is **Chloramphenicol Preparations** whose parents belong to three areas, "Antihistamine Drugs," "Drug Allergy Class," and "DEA Controlled Substance Category."

In the OODB schema, property-introducing areas are treated in the same manner described previously. One *property-introducing* (*area*) *class* is created for each property-introducing area. The properties and subclass relationships of the class are determined by the area's root and its parents, respectively.

For an intersection area, a class [called an *intersection* (*area*) *class*] is defined as we previously defined a property-introducing class for each property-introducing area. However, this class contains *no* intrinsic properties. Instead, it gets all its properties via inheritance—just as its roots do.

The subclass relationships originating with an intersection class are once again determined by the parents of a root. A subtlety that arises here comes from the fact that the parents of one root may reside in areas different from those of the parents of another root. Even so, the union of the parents' sets of properties with respect to one root is always the same as the union with respect to any other. If not, the roots would belong to different areas.

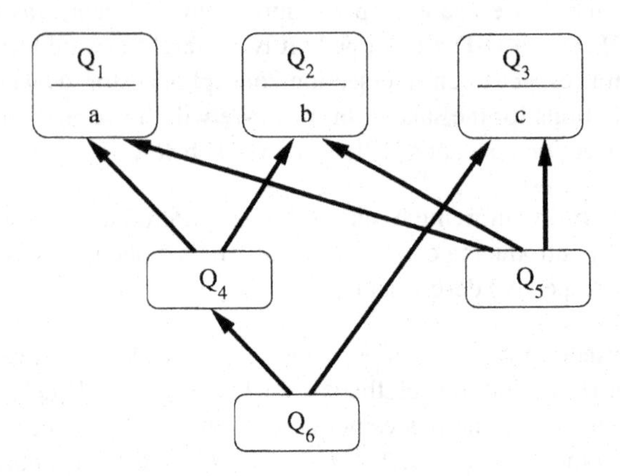


*Figure 7.* Parents of the roots of an intersection area residing in different areas

To illustrate this point, consider the six concepts, $Q_1$ through $Q_6$, shown in Figure 7. Concepts $Q_1$, $Q_2$, and $Q_3$ introduce the attributes $a$, $b$, and $c$, respectively, and therefore serve as the roots of three different property-introducing areas. (In this simplified configuration, they are the only concepts in their respective areas.) $Q_4$ is an intersection concept possessing the properties $a$ and $b$ obtained via inheritance from its parents. The interesting aspect of the figure involves the concepts $Q_5$ and $Q_6$. Both are intersection concepts and possess all three attributes, $a$, $b$, and $c$. Therefore, they are roots of the same intersection area. However, $Q_5$ has the three parents $Q_1$, $Q_2$, and $Q_3$ residing in their own property-introducing areas. Concept $Q_6$ shares the parent $Q_3$ with $Q_5$, but has only one other parent $Q_4$, which, as noted, is an intersection concept. To summarize, we see that the sets of parent areas of an intersection area are not unique. They can differ with respect to its various roots.

Because of this, there are potentially many equivalent subclass configurations (and, hence, OODB schemas) that can be used to represent such an intersection area. The question is: Which of these should be chosen? Our answer is to select the root whose parents collectively reside in the fewest areas and define the subclass relationships with respect to those area classes. This minimizes the required number of subclass relationships.

To demonstrate this, let us refer back to Figure 7. We would select the root $Q_6$ for the intersection area rooted at both $Q_5$ and $Q_6$ because $Q_6$'s parents reside in two areas while $Q_5$'s reside in three. The subclass relationships for this intersection area class would be directed to two classes, one representing the property-introducing area of concept $Q_3$ and the other representing the intersection area rooted at $Q_4$.

In general, the process of determining the subclass relationships for an intersection class is as follows. Let $I$ be an intersection area and let $r_i$ be one of its roots whose parents reside in the fewest different areas.[2] Moreover, let $T_1, T_2, \ldots, T_n$ be all the areas containing at least one of $r_I$'s parents. Then the class *I_Area*, the intersection class for $I$, is defined as a subclass of $T_1$*_Area*, $T_2$*_Area*, through $T_n$*_Area*, the respective area classes of $T_1, T_2, \ldots, T_n$.

As pointed out above, an intersection concept's parents must reside in at least two different areas, so an intersection class will have at least two superclasses. This demonstrates that the OODB schema, for this type of CV, will exhibit multiple inheritance.

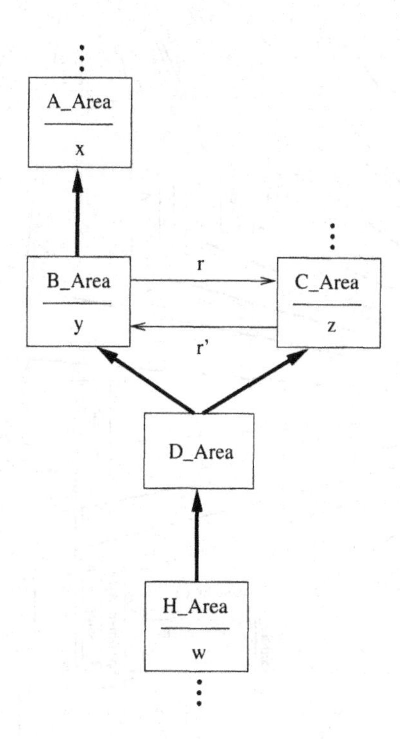


*Figure 8.* Area classes for the areas in Figure 6

To illustrate the schema construction, we show the area classes for the areas from Figure 6 in Figure 8. The ellipses indicate the omission of subclass relationships and additional classes that would appear in an expanded drawing. The three classes, *A_Area*, *B_Area*, and *C_Area*, are defined as discussed previously. Each is a property-introducing class. The class *D_Area* is an intersection class representing the intersection area containing the four concepts, **D**, **E**, **F**, and **G**. Both **D** and **E** are roots of the area and are thus viable designations for it. The name *D_Area* was chosen because **D** appears first in a scan of the area. The class does not have any intrinsic properties. It is a subclass of *B_Area* and *C_Area* because **D**'s parents (as well as **E**'s) belong to the areas $B$ and $C$. *H_Area* is a property-introducing class which introduces the attribute $w$ and is a subclass of *D_Area*.

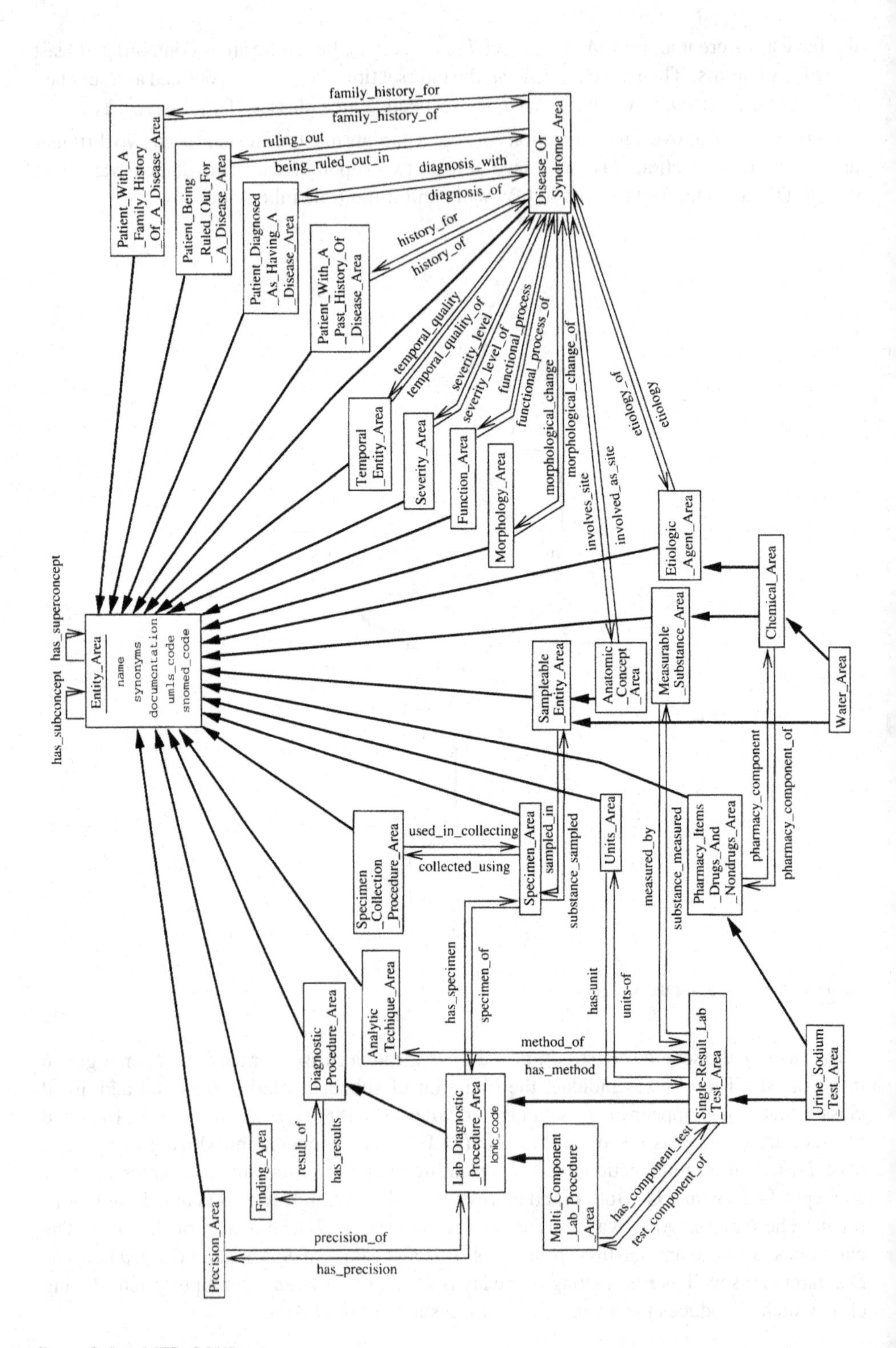


*Figure 9.* InterMED-OOVR schema

In Figure 9, we show the entire InterMED-OOVR schema comprising a total of 28 area classes and 30 subclass relationships. Of the 28 classes, 26 are property-introducing classes and 2 are intersection classes. One of the intersection classes is *Water_Area* which is a subclass of *Sampleable_Entity_Area* and *Chemical_Area*. The other is *Urine_Sodium_Test_-Area* which has the parents *Single_Result_Lab_Test_Area* and *Pharmacy_Items_Drugs_and_-Nondrugs_Area*.

The schema for the MED-OOVR contains 90 classes (57 property-introducing classes, 33 intersection classes) and 134 subclass relationships. Due to its large size, it is not convenient to show the entire schema graphically on one page. In Figure 10, we show only the 57 property-introducing classes. In order to save space, we have drawn the properties as numbers. The corresponding property names can be found in Figure 11. Figure 12 contains all the property-introducing classes (with all properties omitted) as well as the following six intersection classes: *Antihistamine_Drugs_Area*, *Chloramphenicol_Preparations_Area*, *Organism_Area*, *Wucheria_Bancrofti_Area*, *Black_Piedra_Area*, and *Abnormal_Finding_in_Body_Substance_Area*. It should be noted that it is possible for one intersection class to be a subclass of another intersection class. This is demonstrated by three of the intersection classes, *Chloramphenicol_Preparations_Area*, *Wucheria_Bancrofti_Area*, and *Black_Piedra_Area*. Moreover, *Black_Piedra_Area* is two levels below the intersection class *Organism_Area*. Note also that *Chloramphenicol_Preparations_Area* has three parents.

An important aspect of our methodology is the compactness of the resultant OODB schema. For the InterMED, which contains about 2,500 concepts, the schema has merely 28 area classes—about an 80-to-1 reduction. The MED contains approximately 48,000 concepts and has a schema of 90 classes—about a 500-to-1 ratio! Additionally, we find a slow growth rate for the schemas with respect to the size of the source CVs. The content of the MED is nineteen times larger than that of the InterMED, yet its schema is only about three times the size.

In [16], we showed how the compactness of the schema helped a vocabulary administrator uncover mistakes that had been introduced into the MED. We also discussed how this representation can be used as a tool for comprehending the content of a CV. In fact, deriving an OODB schema for a CV was helpful for us both by the process and the result. The process of finding a schema gave us a source for asking intelligent questions about the vocabulary, the answers to which added insights to our comprehension of its knowledge content. The result, the schema itself, is a knowledge-rich abstraction that allows us to split the comprehension process into two steps. In the first step, a person studying the schema gets a good understanding of the CV's overall structure. In the second step, a person using the schema as a road map can then advance to studying selected areas of the CV in detail. In summary, a schema adds a valuable layer of abstraction on top of the large and complex content of a CV. We have built a program that utilizes this separation of CV and schema along with what we call "analogical forms" to provide an enhanced interface to CVs [18]. Using this program, a traversal of the CV can begin at the schema level and continue until the proper class is identified; at that point, the traversal can proceed at the concept level. Further abstraction of a CV can be achieved by partitioning the set of concepts of an area class into smaller units, as suggested in [17].

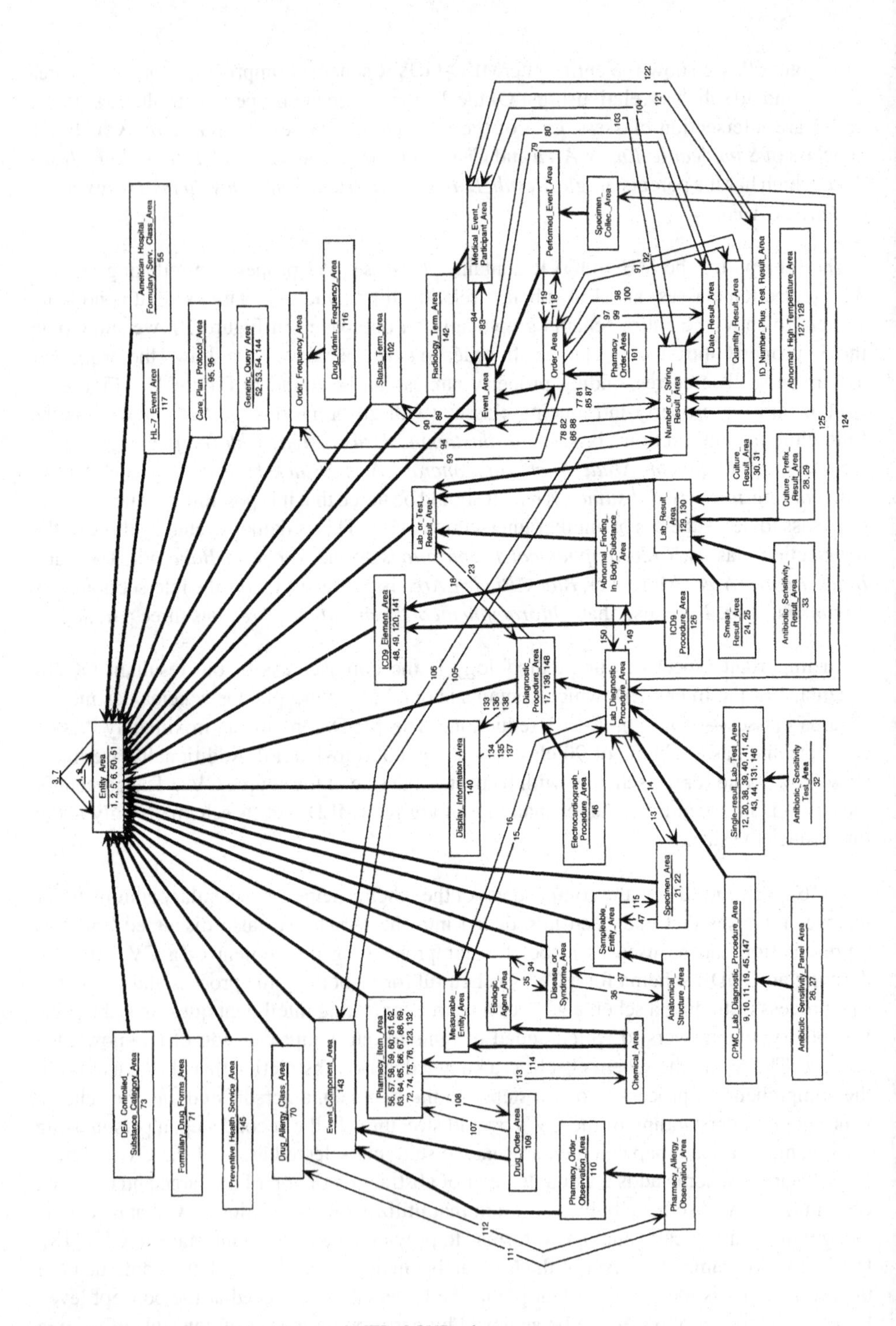


*Figure 10.* Property-introducing classes of MED-OOVR schema

| | | | | | |
|---|---|---|---|---|---|
| 1: | umls_code | 2: | name | 3: | has_subconcept |
| 4: | has_superconcept | 5: | synonyms | 6: | print_name |
| 7: | has_part | 8: | part_of | 9: | cpmc_lab_proc_code |
| 10: | service_code | 11: | cpmc_unit_names | 12: | cpmc_lab_test_names |
| 13: | specimen_of | 14: | specimen | 15: | measured_by |
| 16: | substance_measured | 17: | units | 18: | result_of_tests |
| 19: | cpmc_lab_proc_name | 20: | cpmc_lab_test_code | 21: | cpmc_lab_spec_code |
| 22: | cpmc_lab_spec_name | 23: | result_type | 24: | cpmc_smear_code |
| 25: | cpmc_smear_name | 26: | cpmc_panel_code | 27: | cpmc_panel_name |
| 28: | cpmc_prefix_code | 29: | cpmc_prefix_name | 30: | cpmc_result_code |
| 31: | cpmc_result_name | 32: | cpmc_sensitivity_name | 33: | cpmc_sensitivity_result_name |
| 34: | etiology | 35: | causes_diseases | 36: | site |
| 37: | site_of_diseases | 38: | normal_value | 39: | low_normal_value |
| 40: | high_normal_value | 41: | male_low_normal_value | 42: | male_high_normal_value |
| 43: | female_low_normal_value | 44: | female_high_normal_value | 45: | normal_ranges_text |
| 46: | cpmc_ecg_name | 47: | substance_sampled | 48: | icd9_code |
| 49: | icd9_entry_code | 50: | main_mesh | 51: | supplementary_mesh |
| 52: | question_type | 53: | english_question | 54: | brs_question |
| 55: | ahfs_class_code | 56: | dose_strength_units | 57: | dose_strength_number |
| 58: | formulary_name | 59: | short_formulary_name | 60: | formulary_code |
| 61: | drug_trade_name | 62: | drug_generic_name | 63: | drug_manufacturer |
| 64: | drug_rx_vs_otc | 65: | drug_form_code | 66: | drug_floor_stock |
| 67: | drug_route | 68: | drug_in_formulary | 69: | drug_volume |
| 70: | allergy_class_code | 71: | drug_description | 72: | drug_category |
| 73: | dea_code | 74: | drug_specifier | 75: | drug_generic_code |
| 76: | drug_interaction_codes | 77: | event_id | 78: | event_id_of |
| 79: | event_date | 80: | event_date_of | 81: | event_patient_id |
| 82: | event_patient_id_of | 83: | event_participant | 84: | participant_of |
| 85: | event_organization | 86: | event_organization_of | 87: | event_location |
| 88: | event_location_of | 89: | event_status | 90: | status_of |
| 91: | order_quantity | 92: | order_quantity_of | 93: | order_frequency |
| 94: | order_frequency_of | 95: | protocol_name | 96: | protocol_short_name |
| 97: | order_start_date | 98: | order_start_date_of | 99: | order_stop_date |
| 100: | order_stop_date_of | 101: | pharmacy_order_code | 102: | status_code |
| 103: | participant_id | 104: | participant_id_of | 105: | order_value |
| 106: | order_value_of | 107: | ordered_drug | 108: | ordered_in |
| 109: | drug_role_code | 110: | pharmacy_observation_code | 111: | observed_allergy |
| 112: | allergy_observed_in | 113: | pharmaceutic_component | 114: | pharmaceutic_component_of |
| 115: | sampled_by | 116: | admin_frequency_abbrev | 117: | hl7_event_code |
| 118: | event_object | 119: | object_of_event | 120: | old_icd9_code |
| 121: | participant_name | 122: | participant_name_of | 123: | drug_id |
| 124: | collected_for | 125: | collected_by | 126: | cpt4_code |
| 127: | lower_limit_for_input | 128: | upper_limit_for_input | 129: | lab_message_code |
| 130: | lab_message_text | 131: | cpmc_long_test_name | 132: | drug_alert_code |
| 133: | has_default_displays | 134: | default_display_for | 135: | displays_elements_of |
| 136: | elements_displayed_by | 137: | has_display_parameters | 138: | is_display_parameter_of |
| 139: | has_test_display_class_name | 140: | display_parameter_order | 141: | icd9_name |
| 142: | cpmc_radiology_code | 143: | event_component_display_name | 144: | query_fillers |
| 145: | preventive_health_name | 146: | lab_alt_test_name | 147: | lab_alt_proc_name |
| 148: | has_proc_display_class_name | 149: | defined_by_test | 150: | defines_abnormal_finding |

*Figure 11.* Legend for properties of MED-OOVR schema in Figure 10

## 4. Program for Generating the OODB Representation of a CV

We have used our methodology to transform two existing medical CVs, the InterMED and the MED, into object-oriented representations. The methodology can be applied not only to medical CVs but to any semantic network-based vocabulary, as long as it satisfies the "uniqueness of property introduction" rule discussed earlier. Both OODB representations, called, respectively, the InterMED-OOVR and the MED-OOVR, are currently up and running on top of the ONTOS DB/Explorer OODB management system. The creation of each was done automatically by a program called the *OOVR Generator*, which can be used to convert any source CV into its equivalent OODB form.

In this section, we describe the overall architecture of the OOVR Generator. We will first present the assumed format of the source CV. We will then go on to discuss the components of the OOVR Generator's functionality.

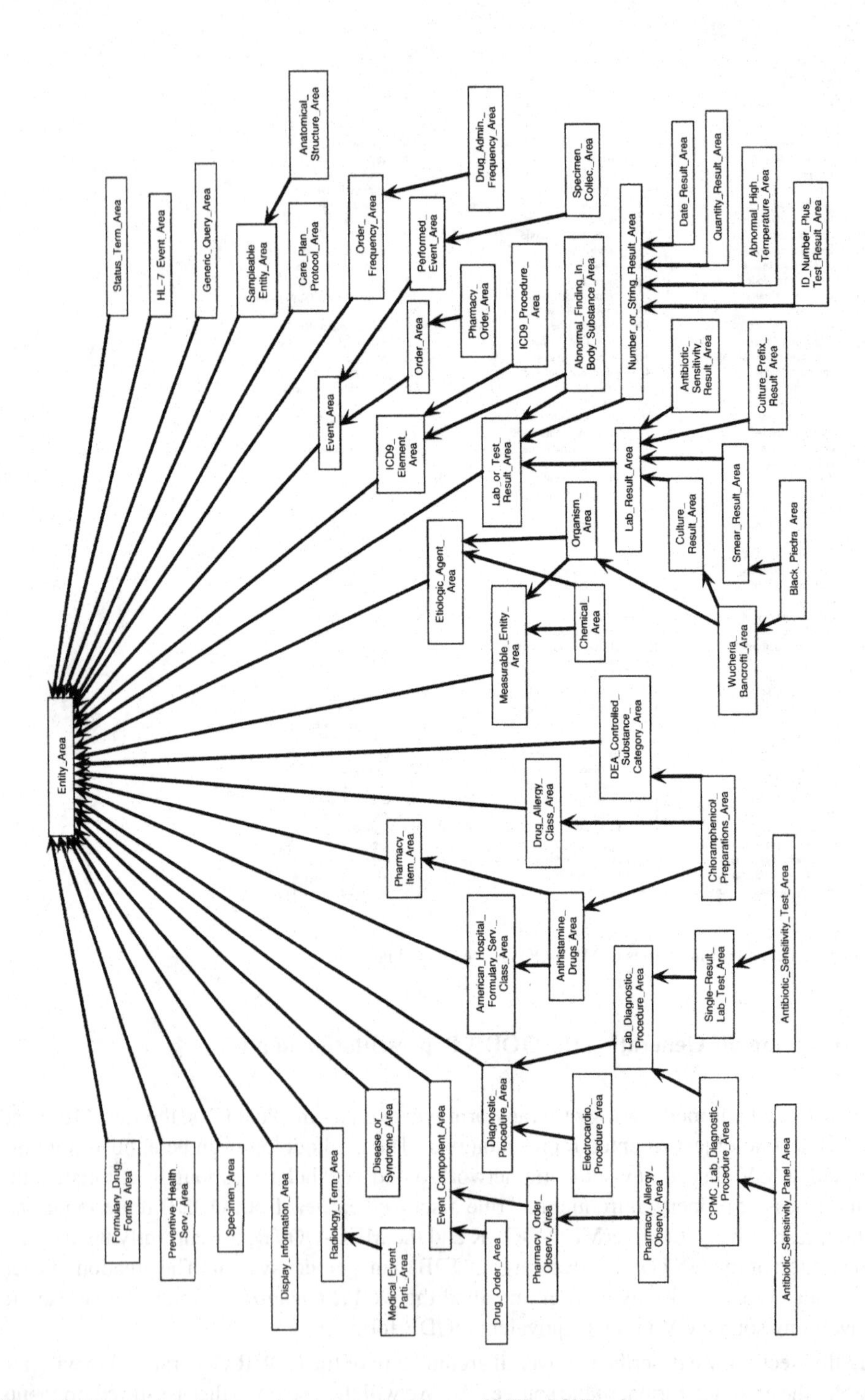


*Figure 12.* Property-introducing and six intersection classes of MED-OOVR schema

### *4.1. Format of the Source CV*

Various CVs can be assumed to be stored in different formats on disk. However, we will expect that a CV that is to be processed by our technique has a representation as a pair of text files, each having a specific syntax. If the desired source CV does not conform to this requirement, then it will first need to be converted. For this purpose, we include a *Preprocessor* module in the architecture of the OOVR Generator (see Figure 13). This portion may need to be modified for different CVs. To illustrate the necessary format, we will be referring to the InterMED, from which it was originally gleaned. The MED also employs this representation.

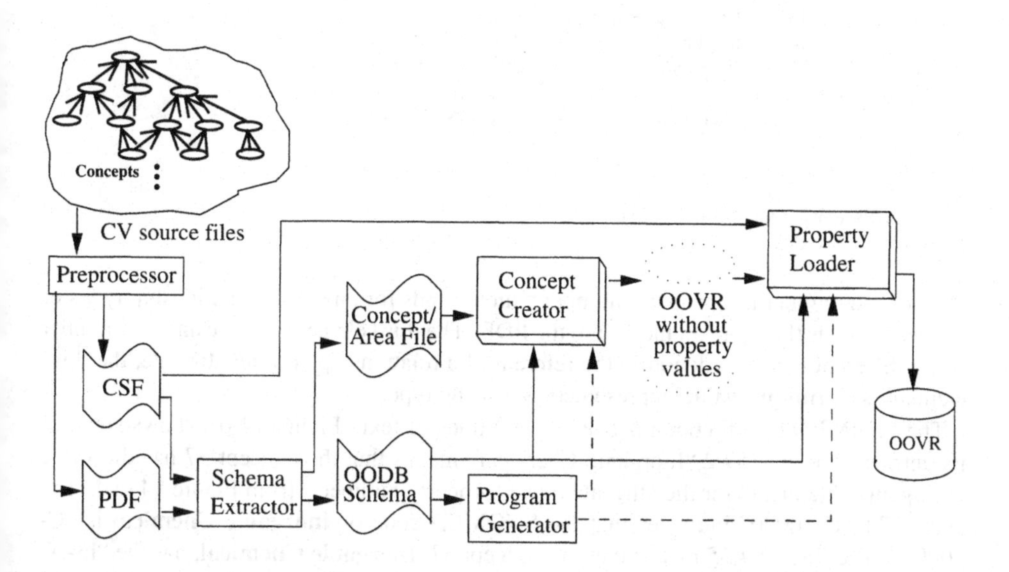


*Figure 13.* Architecture of the OOVR Generator

The two text files making up the disk-resident format of a CV are referred to as the *Property Definition File* (*PDF*) and the *Concept Specification File* (*CSF*). The PDF describes all the attributes and relationship types of the CV. Every attribute (or relationship type) is described by one line in the PDF. Each line is a triple whose first component is the property's number, which is assigned to a property in order to simplify references to it. The second component is the property's name; the third component is the number of the concept which introduces the property.

There are 51 lines in the InterMED's PDF. Figure 14 (a) shows an excerpt of the file.[3] Note that the fields of a line are separated by commas. The MED's PDF contains 150 lines.

The second file, the CSF, describes all the details of the concepts' properties. Each line denotes the value for one property of some concept. A line in this file is also a triple. The first element is a concept number, uniquely identifying one of the concepts in the CV.

| (a) InterMED PDF | (b) InterMED CSF |
|---|---|
| 1, umls-code, 1 | 1,1,"T071" |
| 2, name, 1 | 1,2,"Entity" |
| 3, descendant-of, 1 | 3,2,"Diagnostic Procedure" |
| 4, is-a, 1 | 4,2,"Laboratory Diagnostic Procedure" |
| 5, synonyms, 1 | 28,2,"Finding" |
| 6, print-name, 1 | 35,2,"Chemical Viewed Structurally" |
| 7, documentation, 1 | 37,2,"Inorganic Chemical" |
| 8, snomed-code, 1 | 37,4,35 |
| 9, has-result, 3 | 37,8,"C-10090" |
| 10, result-of, 28 | 37,14,7 |
| 11, has-specimen, 4 | 38,1,"T106" |
| 12, specimen-of, 29 | 38,2,"Element or Elemental Ion" |
| 13, substance-measured, 5 | 38,4,37 |
| 14, measured-by, 30 | 39,1,"C0037473" |
| 15, has-precision, 5 | 39,2,"Sodium Ion" |

*Figure 14.* Excerpts of InterMED source files

The second number is a property number which stands for one of the relationship types or attributes and is therefore an index into the PDF. The third element may be another number (for a different concept) denoting the referent of a relationship. For an attribute, the third element is a primitive value, represented as a string type.

The InterMED's CSF contains over 32,000 lines of text. Figure 14 (b) shows some of its entries. The line 37,2,"Inorganic Chemical" means that the concept 37 has the value "Inorganic Chemical" for the attribute *name* [property number 2 from Figure 14 (a)]. The entry 37,8,"C-10090" indicates that the SNOMED code of **Inorganic Chemical** is "C-10090." The line 37,4,35 means that the concept 37, **Inorganic Chemical**, has the "IS-A" relationship (property number 4) to concept 35, **Chemical Viewed Structurally**. The MED's CSF is quite a bit larger than that of the InterMED because the MED contains about nineteen times as many concepts having many more properties. In total, the MED's CSF has around 1,000,000 lines.

### 4.2. *Architecture of the OOVR Generator*

Figure 13 shows the overall architecture of the OOVR Generator. The OOVR Generator is a "second-order" process, with some of its modules being constructed by other modules during run-time. In the figure, we are using the following graphical conventions. A box represents a program module. A box with depth indicates that the module is generated by another module. The creation of such a module $A$ by another module $B$ is depicted by a dashed arrow from $B$ to $A$. Ordinary arrows indicate the flow of data between modules either as files (wavy boxes) or databases (cylinders).

As we see from the figure, the OOVR Generator consists of five modules: *Preprocessor*, *Schema Extractor*, *Program Generator*, *Concept Creator*, and *Property Loader*. The Preprocessor is the only module which, as noted above, is CV-dependent. Hence, for a CV with a different file format from the InterMED's, it would need to be modified.

The Schema Extractor is the first module to process the source CV. Its task is to carry out the area-partitioning and produce the appropriate OODB schema (as described in the previous section). It takes as its input both the PDF and the CSF. The output consists of two items, a "Concept/Area File" and the actual OODB schema for the OOVR. The Concept/Area File simply holds the mapping between the concepts of the CV and the areas derived from the partitioning process. Effectively, it is a two-column table, where the first column contains the concept names, and the second holds the associated area (class) names.

Presently, the OODB schema created by the Schema Extractor is specified in the DDL of the ONTOS system. Therefore, an OOVR will be an ONTOS database. We are in the process of updating the Schema Extractor such that it will build a schema specification in the portable Object Definition Language (ODL) proposed by the Object Database Management Group (ODMG) [5]. This would make our software independent of the back-end OODB system, which then could be any one that is ODMG-compliant.

The Program Generator, as its name suggests, generates two architectural modules (as marked by dashed arrows in Figure 13): the Concept Creator and the Property Loader (drawn as boxes with depth). As we see, to do its work, the Program Generator requires the OODB schema produced by the Schema Extractor. Before describing why the Program Generator module is needed, let us discuss the details of the two modules that it generates.

The Concept Creator and the Property Loader together populate the OOVR. The Concept Creator first instantiates all concepts. That is, it creates one object in the OOVR for each concept in the source CV. The class of each object is determined by the Concept/Area File, which contains the concept-to-area mapping that we have described in the previous section. Note that the OOVR has all its concepts when the Concept Creator finishes, but none of those concepts has any property values (as indicated by the "phantom" OOVR having the dashed cylinder in the picture). This situation is rectified by the Property Loader which provides the concepts with the values of all their attributes and relationships. It obtains these from the CSF that comes directly from the Preprocessor stage.

The reason that the process of populating the OOVR is divided into two steps is because relationships are concept-to-concept (or object-to-object) references. In order to establish a relationship at a given object, the referenced objects must already exist. However, this may not be the case while the Concept Creator is carrying out its task. Therefore, it is necessary to defer the establishment of relationships until after all concepts have been created. So, in our architecture, Concept Creator first creates all the objects, and then Property Loader connects them via the appropriate relationships (and assigns their attribute values, as well).

The need for the Program Generator is dictated by the differences in structure that one finds among CVs. While we have set forth general vocabulary characteristics in Section 2, different CVs will certainly exhibit diverse properties and property introduction patterns. In other words, different CVs will have different OODB schemas! Both the Concept Creator and the Property Loader utilize the class definitions contained in the schema to perform their functions in the task of populating the OOVR. The distinctions in the class definitions (e.g., the diversity of class names, numbers of properties, and so on) from CV to CV require that the declaration sections of both these modules be created anew for each source CV. Fortunately, the modules' overall forms have been captured as templates, and the process of generating them is automated. As mentioned above, this leaves only the Preprocessor open to changes for different CVs.

The complexity of the algorithm carried out by the OOVR Generator is on the order of the total number of properties occurring within the CV. Specifically, let *Attr* be the set of all occurrences of attributes in the CV. Likewise, let *Rel* be the set of all occurrences of relationships. Then, the complexity is $O(|Attr| + |Rel|)$. We omit the details of the analysis for the sake of brevity. It will be noted that:

$$|Attr| + |Rel| = \sum_{x \in \mathrm{CV}} |P(x)| = \text{Number of lines in the CSF.}$$

where $|P(x)|$ is the number of properties of the concept $x$. Thus, the complexity is on the order of the CSF's size.

## 5. Conclusions

Controlled vocabularies (CVs) organize large groups of concepts into cogent bodies of knowledge which can be used to unify and integrate different, often independently created, applications with idiosyncratic terminologies. The semantic network has proven to be a viable modeling vehicle for CVs. However, designers, administrators, and users of CVs can be overwhelmed by the inherent complexity and size of typical vocabulary networks. In addition, semantic-network processing tools have not enjoyed significant commercial acceptance. This lack of availability is an obstacle to the wide-spread utilization of CVs.

In this paper, we have addressed these problems by presenting a methodology for converting a semantic network-based CV into the form of an object-oriented database (OODB), called an Object-Oriented Vocabulary Repository (OOVR). The OODB schema resulting from this process is a valuable layer of abstraction. It offers a high-level view of the structure of the knowledge which can help the various classes of users in designing, managing, and utilizing a CV more effectively. In fact, in previous work we have described how the schema of the MED, a large CV from the medical domain, uncovered problems in the MED's original design. This eventually led to improvements in the MED's knowledge content. We have also constructed a Web-based, CV interface centered around the two view-levels of an OOVR (i.e., the schema level and the concept level) in order to provide enhanced access. At the moment, we are investigating additional, useful levels of abstraction that would enable a user to choose different amounts of detail.

In formally defining our methodology, we have utilized a variety of notions including that of property-introducing concept and the completely new notions of intersection concept, direct property-introducing descendant, and direct intersection descendant. Using these, it was possible to precisely describe how the CV is partitioned into areas, how object classes corresponding to these areas are defined, and which properties need to be assigned to these classes to capture the contents of the semantic-network input.

To complement the formal aspects of our methodology, we have built a program called the OOVR Generator which automatically carries out the methodology. We discussed the architectural details of this program. Interestingly, the OOVR Generator is a "second-order" process, with some of its modules being constructed by other modules during execution. Overall, the OOVR takes as its input a CV contained in two text files, called the Property Description File and the Concept Specification File, and produces a fully functioning OOVR. No human intervention in the form of database modeling or populating is required.

To demonstrate our methodology, we have applied it to the mid-sized InterMED and the very large MED, two CVs from the medical domain. Indeed, we have used the OOVR Generator to produce the OOVRs for both of these. They are currently up and running on top of ONTOS. The InterMED-OOVR is on the Web [43].

While our demonstrations focused on medical CVs, let us emphasize that our methodology is completely general. It works for any semantic-network CV in any subject area, as long as it is possible to map the CV into the PDF and CSF formats which we have described, and as long as the "uniqueness of property introduction" rule is satisfied. The OOVR Generator contains a module, called the Preprocessor, which performs any necessary mapping into the required file formats and which has to be rewritten for different semantic-network formalisms. Other than that, the OOVR Generator is completely general. In summary, our approach will help future CV builders to implement large, understandable, maintainable vocabularies, running on top of well supported database systems.

## Acknowledgments

We would like to thank Huanying Gu and Jim Cimino for their helpful discussions and insights. We also thank Boris Harmeyer for creating the MED-OOVR figures.

## Notes

1. Some typographical conventions: A bold face font will be used for concepts' terms. Properties of concepts will appear in italics and will be written strictly in lowercase letters. Object classes will also be written in italics. These class names, however, will start with uppercase letters.
2. There may be more than one such root. In that case, the choice is made arbitrarily.
3. The actual InterMED PDF contains some additional fields that are not relevant to the conversion process. These are removed by the Preprocessor.

## References

1. American Society of Hospital Pharmacists, Bethesda, MD. *American Hospital Formulary Service Drug Information*, 1997. Updated annually.
2. R. J. Brachman. On the epistemological status of semantic networks. In N. V. Findler, editor, *Associative Networks: Representation and Use of Knowledge by Computers*, pages 3–50. Academic Press, Inc., New York, NY, 1979.
3. S. K. Card. User limits and the VDT computer interface (excerpt). In R. M. Baecker and W. A. S. Buxton, editors, *Readings in Human-Computer Interaction*, pages 180–191. Morgan Kaufmann Publishers, Inc., Los Altos, CA, 1987.
4. M. J. Carey, D. J. DeWitt, J. E. Richardson, and E. J. Shekita. Storage management for objects in EXODUS. In W. Kim and F. H. Lochovsky, editors, *Object-Oriented Concepts, Databases, and Applications*, pages 341–369. ACM Press, New York, NY, 1989.
5. R. G. G. Cattell and D. K. Barry, editors. *The Object Database Standard: ODMG 2.0.* Morgan Kaufmann Publishers, Inc., San Francisco, CA, 1997.

6. P. P.-S. Chen. The Entity-Relationship Model: Toward a unified view of data. *ACM Trans. Database Syst.*, 1(1):9–36, 1976.
7. J. J. Cimino. Personal communication, 1997.
8. J. J. Cimino, P. D. Clayton, G. Hripcsak, and S. B. Johnson. Knowledge-based approaches to the maintenance of a large controlled medical terminology. *JAMIA*, 1(1):35–50, 1994.
9. J. J. Cimino, G. Hripcsak, S. B. Johnson, and P. D. Clayton. Designing an introspective, multipurpose, controlled medical vocabulary. In *Proc. Thirteenth Annual Symposium on Computer Applications in Medical Care*, pages 513–517, Washington, DC, Nov. 1989.
10. College of American Pathologists, Skokie, IL. *Systematized Nomenclature of Medicine*, second edition, 1982.
11. O. Deux et al. The $O_2$ system. *Commun. ACM*, 34(10):34–48, Oct. 1991.
12. D. H. Fischer. Consistency rules and triggers for thesauri. *Int. Classif.*, 18(4):212–225, 1991.
13. D. H. Fischer. Consistency rules and triggers for multilingual terminology. In *Proc. TKE'93, Terminology and Knowledge Engineering*, pages 333–342, 1993.
14. GemStone Systems, Inc. URL: http://www.gemstone.com.
15. C. A. Goble, A. J. Glowinski, W. A. Nolan, and A. L. Rector. A descriptive semantic formalism for medicine. In *Proc. 9th ICDE*, pages 624–631, Vienna, Austria, 1993.
16. H. Gu, J. Cimino, M. Halper, J. Geller, and Y. Perl. Utilizing OODB schema modeling for vocabulary management. In J. Cimino, editor, *Proc. 1996 AMIA Annual Fall Symposium*, pages 274–278, Washington, DC, Oct. 1996.
17. H. Gu, Y. Perl, J. Geller, M. Halper, J. Cimino, and M. Singh. Partitioning a vocabulary's IS-A hierarchy into trees. In D. R. Masys, editor, *Proc. 1997 AMIA Annual Fall Symposium*, pages 630–634, Nashville, TN, Oct. 1997.
18. M. Halper, R. Galnares, J. Geller, and Y. Perl. An analogical, Web-based interface to an OODB medical vocabulary. In preparation.
19. M. Hammer and D. McLeod. Database description with SDM: A semantic database model. *ACM Trans. Database Syst.*, 6(3):351–386, 1981.
20. R. Hull and R. King. Semantic database modeling: Survey, applications, and research issues. *ACM Comput. Surv.*, 19(3):201–260, Sept. 1987.
21. N. Ide, J. L. Maitre, and J. Véronis. Outline of a model for lexical databases. *Information Processing and Management*, 29(2):159–186, 1993.
22. P. D. Karp, K. Myers, and T. Gruber. The generic frame protocol. In *Proc. IJCAI-95*, pages 768–774, Montreal, Canada, 1995.
23. P. D. Karp and S. M. Paley. Knowledge representation in the large. In *Proc. IJCAI-95*, pages 751–758, Montreal, Canada, 1995.
24. M. Kifer, W. Kim, and Y. Sagiv. Querying object-oriented databases. In *Proc. 1992 ACM SIGMOD Conference on Management of Data*, San Diego, CA, June 1992.
25. W. Kim and F. H. Lochovsky, editors. *Object-Oriented Concepts, Databases, and Applications*. ACM Press, New York, NY, 1989.
26. C. Lamb, G. Landis, J. Orenstein, and D. Weinreb. The ObjectStore database system. *Commun. ACM*, 34(10):50–63, Oct. 1991.
27. F. Lehmann. Semantic networks. In [28], pages 1–50.
28. F. Lehmann, editor. *Semantic Networks in Artificial Intelligence*. Pergamon Press, Tarrytown, NY, 1992.
29. D. B. Lenat and R. V. Guha. *Building Large Knowledge-Based Systems: Representation and Inference in the Cyc Project*. Addison-Wesley Publishing Co., Inc., Reading, MA, 1990.
30. L. Liu, M. Halper, H. Gu, J. Geller, and Y. Perl. Modeling a vocabulary in an object-oriented database. In K. Barker and M. T. Özsu, editors, *CIKM-96, Proc. 5th Int'l Conference on Information and Knowledge Management*, pages 179–188, Rockville, MD, Nov. 1996.
31. E. Mays, C. Apte, J. Griesmer, and J. Kastner. Experience with K-Rep: An object-centered knowledge representation language. In *Proc. IEEE AI Application Conference*, San Diego, CA, Mar. 1988.
32. G. A. Miller. The magical number seven, plus or minus two: Some limits on our capacity for processing information. *Psych. Rev.*, 63, 1956.
33. G. A. Miller. WordNet: A lexical database for English. *Commun. ACM*, 38(11):39–41, 1995.
34. W. Möhr and L. Rostek. TEDI: An object-oriented terminology editor. In *Proc. TKE'93, Terminology and Knowledge Engineering*, pages 363–374, 1993.

35. J. Mylopoulos, A. Borgida, M. Jarke, and M. Koubarakis. Telos: Representing knowledge about information systems. *TOIS*, 8(4):325–362, 1990.
36. J. Mylopoulos, V. Chaudhri, D. Plexousakis, A. Shrufi, and T. Topaloglou. Building knowledge base management systems: A progress report. Technical Report DKBS-TR-94-4, Department of Computer Science, University of Toronto, 1994.
37. The National Drug Code Directory. URL: http://www.fda.gov/cder/ndc/index.htm.
38. N. F. Noy and C. D. Hafner. The state of the art in ontology design: A survey and comparative review. *AI Magazine*, 18(3):53–74, Fall 1997.
39. Welcome to ODI. URL: http://www.odi.com.
40. D. E. Oliver, E. H. Shortliffe, and InterMed Collaboratory. Collaborative model development for vocabulary and guidelines. In J. Cimino, editor, *Proc. 1996 AMIA Annual Fall Symposium*, page 826, Washington, DC, Oct. 1996.
41. ONTOS Home Page. URL: http://www.ontos.com.
42. ONTOS, Inc. Lowell, MA. *ONTOS DB 3.1 Reference Manual*, 1995.
43. The OOVR Browser.
URL: http://object.njit.edu:2000/~newoohvr/JBI/INTERMED/InterTerms.html.
44. Object Technology by Ardent Software ($O_2$ System).
URL: http://www.ardentsoftware.com/object/index.html.
45. S. C. Shapiro and W. J. Rapaport. The SNePS family. In [28], pages 243–275.
46. E. H. Shortliffe, G. O. Barnett, J. Cimino, R. A. Greenes, S. M. Huff, and V. L. Patel. Collaborative medical informatics research using the Internet and the World Wide Web. In J. Cimino, editor, *Proc. 1996 AMIA Annual Fall Symposium*, pages 125–129, Washington, DC, Oct. 1996.
47. V. Soloviev. An overview of three commercial object-oriented database management systems: ONTOS, ObjectStore, and $O_2$. *SIGMOD Record*, 21(1):93–104, Mar. 1992.
48. J. F. Sowa. *Principles of Semantic Networks, Explorations in the Representation of Knowledge*. Morgan Kaufmann Publishers, Inc., San Mateo, CA, 1991.
49. U. S. Department of Health and Human Services, National Institutes of Health, National Library of Medicine. *Unified Medical Language System*, 1996.
50. United States National Center for Health Statistics, Washington, DC. *International Classification of Diseases: Ninth Revision, with Clinical Modifications*, 1980.
51. P. Valduriez, S. Khoshafian, and G. Copeland. Implementation techniques of complex objects. In *Proc. VLDB '86*, pages 101–109, Kyoto, Japan, Aug. 1986.
52. Versant. URL: http://www.versant.com.
53. W. A. Woods. What's in a link: Foundations for semantic networks. In R. J. Brachman and H. J. Levesque, editors, *Readings in Knowledge Representation*, pages 218–241. Morgan Kaufmann Publishers, Inc., San Mateo, CA, 1985.
54. S. B. Zdonik and D. Maier, editors. *Readings in Object-Oriented Database Systems*. Morgan Kaufmann Publishers, Inc., San Mateo, CA, 1990.
55. J. Zhang. Application of OODB and SGML techniques in text database: An electronic dictionary system. *SIGMOD Record*, 24(1):3–8, Mar. 1995.

Distributed and Parallel Databases, 7, 67–98 (1999)


# A Discovery-Based Approach to Database Ontology Design*

SILVANA CASTANO castano@dsi.unimi.it
*University of Milano - Dipartimento di Scienze dell'Informazione - via Comelico 39 - 20135 Milano - ITALY*

VALERIA DE ANTONELLIS deantone@ing.unibs.it, deantone@elet.polimi.it
*University of Brescia - Dipartimento di Elettronica per l'Automazione - via Branze 38 - 25123 Brescia - ITALY*

*Received April 1, 1998; Accepted June 10, 1998*

**Recommended by:** Athman Bouguettaya

**Abstract.** In this paper, we introduce an approach to task-driven ontology design which is based on information discovery from database schemas. Techniques for semi-automatically discovering terms and relationships used in the information space, denoting concepts, their properties and links are proposed, which are applied in two stages. At the first stage, the focus is on the discovery of heterogeneity/ambiguity of data representations in different schemas. For this purpose, schema elements are compared according to defined comparison features and similarity coefficients are evaluated. This stage produces a set of candidates for unification into ontology concepts. At the second stage, decisions are made on which candidates to unify into concepts and on how to relate concepts by semantic links. Ontology concepts and links can be accessed according to different perspectives, so that the ontology can serve different purposes, such as, providing a search space for powerful mechanisms for concept location, setting a basis for query formulation and processing, and establishing a reference for recognizing terminological relationships between elements in different schemas.

**Keywords:** Ontology design, Similarity techniques, Schema analysis and clustering, Distributed and heterogeneous databases.

## 1. Introduction

The continuously increasing number of multiple distributed heterogeneous and Web-based information systems makes the accessibility and effective exploitation of published information essential problems. In this framework, it is important to provide tools and services for information sharing and exchange. The role of ontologies for information sharing has been recognized [16, 28]. Domain and task-driven ontologies have been developed to facilitate communication and agreement among multiple distributed sources/agents [18]. Specifically, "in a task-driven design approach, the focus is on the needs of a task such as database merging or integration of business enterprise models. The resulting ontology may contain only knowledge that was needed for performing a task and, hence, may not cover the domain fully [28]."

The role of ontologies for databases and information systems in a given domain is to organize the knowledge about database elements (e.g., tables, classes), often ambiguous or

* This research has been partially funded by the *Metodologie e Tecnologie per la Gestione di Dati e Processi su Reti Internet e Intranet - MURST ex-40%* project, and partially by the Information System Authority for Public Administration (AIPA).

heterogeneous in the domain, at a higher abstraction level into concepts and relationships among concepts. This way, an ontology provides an abstract view of the information space that can be exploited by the user for querying several distributed databases in a uniform way, overcoming possible heterogeneity.

In this paper, we present a discovery-based approach to design a task-driven ontology for a set of distributed, independently developed databases. Preliminary definitions of the basic concepts have been presented in [8]. The proposed approach relies on: i) the database conceptual schemas, or metadata, describing the database contents at the intensional level, and ii) mining techniques for the analysis of database schemas for the extraction of ontology concepts and concept links. The proposed techniques are applied in two stages. At the first stage, the focus is on the discovery of heterogeneity/ambiguity among data representations in different schemas. For this purpose, schema elements are compared according to defined comparison features and similarity coefficients are evaluated. This stage produces a set of candidates for unification into ontology concepts. At the second stage, decisions are made on which candidates to unify into concepts and on how to relate concepts by semantic links. The approach has been experimented to construct database ontologies for databases of the italian Central Public Administration in collaboration with the Italian Information Systems Authority for the Public Administration (AIPA).

The paper is organized as follows. In Section 2, we describe the proposed database ontology structure and roles. In Section 3, we describe the two-stage discovery approach for database ontology design. In Section 4, we illustrate techniques for the classification stage, while in Section 5, we present the techniques for the unification stage. In Section 6, we discuss the intended usages of the database ontology. In Section 7, we discuss scalability and maintenance issues. In Section 8, we describe the application of the proposed approach to the construction of database ontologies for two different sets of databases in the Public Administration domain. In Section 9, we make comparison with related work. Finally, in Section 10, we give our concluding remarks.

## 2. Ontology structure and roles

A database ontology is a directed graph where nodes are concepts. Formally, a database ontology $O$ is a pair $O = \langle C, L \rangle$ where:

- $C$ is the set of concepts. A concept $C_q \in C$ is defined as 4-uple of the form: $$\langle n(C_q), P(C_q), FP(C_q), \overline{Cl}_q^* \rangle$$

  where:

  - $n(C_q)$ is the name of the concept.
  - $P(C_q)$ is the set of properties of the concept.
  - $FP(C_q)$ is the set of featuring properties of $C_q$, with $FP(C_k) \subseteq P(C_q)$. A featuring property is a property which is salient to characterize $C_q$ with respect to other concepts in the ontology.
  - $\overline{Cl}_q^*$ is a reference to a cluster of schema elements from which $C_q$ is derived. This means that $C_q$ is representative of all elements in the cluster. The symbol '*' denotes optionality.

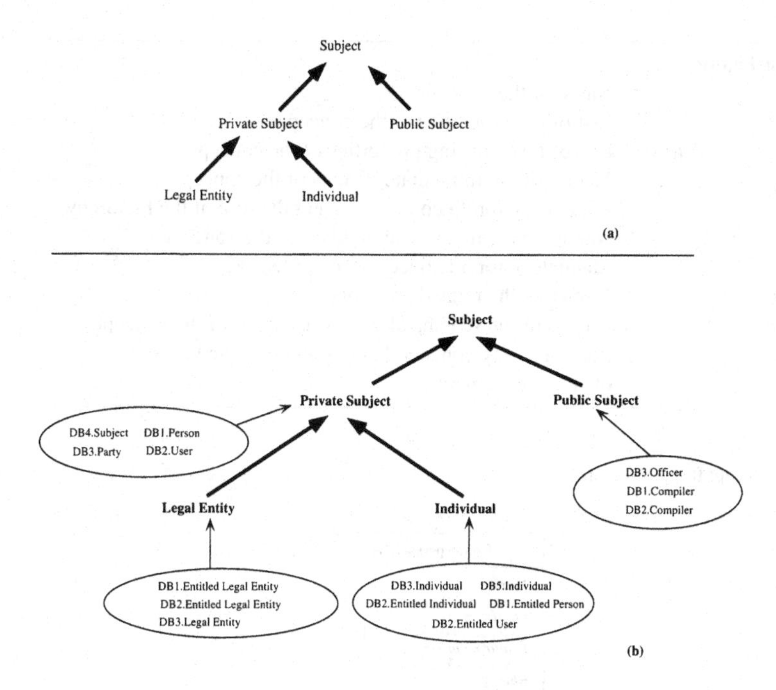


*Figure 1.* A portion of a database ontology for the Land Department databases showing only *kind-of* links (a) and also schema element clusters (b)

- $L$ is a set of links. The following types of links are maintained for concepts in the ontology:
  - *kind-of* links between pairs of concepts to represent the subsumption relationship. A *kind-of* link from concept $C_q$ to concept $C_k$ denotes that $C_k$ subsumes $C_q$.
  - *association* to represent generic semantic relationships that can be established between concepts (e.g., part-of, owns, causes).
  - *instance-of* links between a schema element in $Cl_q$ and $C_q$. An *instance-of* link from a schema element $e_k \in Cl_q$ to a concept $C_q$ denotes that $e_k$ is an instance of $C_q$.

As an example, a simple portion of a database ontology constructed for databases of the Land Department of the Italian the Public Administration is shown in Fig. 1.

***Perspectives.*** Concepts in the ontology can be presented according to different perspectives focusing on different links and properties of concepts. Given a concept $C_q \in C$, the following perspectives can be invoked:

- *Frame perspective*: the structure of $C_q$ describes name and properties of $C_q$ and, in accordance with the different links defined for $C_q$, also its associated concepts and schema elements. The concept frame structure is shown in Fig. 2.

| **Concept Frame** | |
|---|---|
| *Name:* | Name of the concept. |
| *Properties:* | List of the properties of the concept. |
| *Featuring Properties:* | List of the featuring properties of the concept. |
| *Kind-of:* | Names of the immediate parents of the concept. Mandatory for all concepts except the root of the hierarchy. |
| *Subconcepts:* | Names of the immediate children of the concept. Mandatory for all concepts except leaves. |
| *Association:* | Names of the related concepts. |
| *Instances:* | Names of the schema elements instances of the concept. Present in any concept that has an associated cluster of schema elements. |

*Figure 2.* Concept frame structure

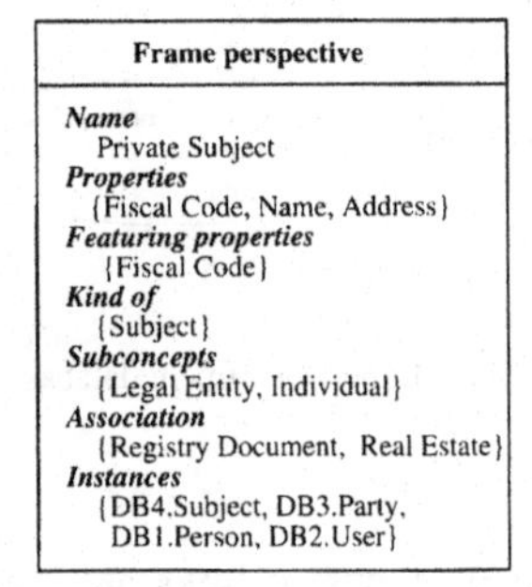


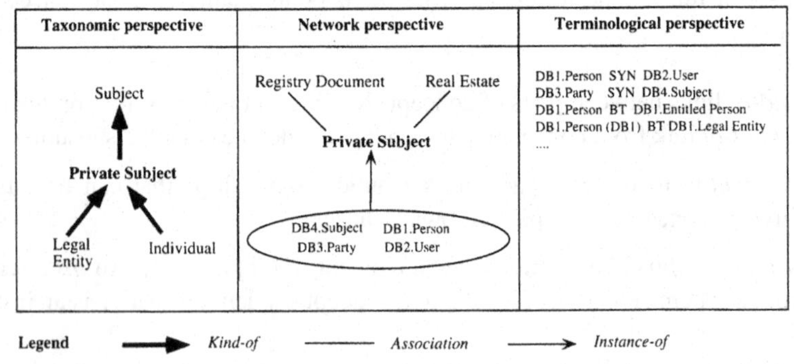


*Figure 3.* Presentation of the concept `Private Subject` according to the different ontology perspectives

- *Taxonomic perspective*: $C_q$ location within the hierarchical organization of concepts is shown, by exploiting the *kind-of* links of $C_q$.

- *Network perspective*: various types of relationships of $C_q$ with other concepts are represented, by exploiting the *association* and *instance of* links of $C_q$.

- *Terminological perspective*: terminological relationships holding for schema elements in the cluster associated with $C_q$ are represented. This perspective exploits an underlying thesaurus where names of schema elements and properties are stored as terms, and a set of binary terminological relationships are maintained between terms. Conventional terminological relationships are maintained in the thesaurus [33], such as *synonymy*, denoted by $SYN$, *hypernymy*, denoted by $BT$ (Broader Terms) and its inverse (Narrower Terms) denoted by $NT$, *positive association*, denoted by $RT$ (Related Terms). The thesaurus is logically organized as an associative network, where nodes correspond to terms and labeled edges between nodes represent terminological relationships. The label $l$ associated with an edge is a triplet $l = \langle \Re, \sigma_{\Re}, k \rangle$, where $\Re \in \{SYN, BT/NT, RT\}$ is the type of relationship, $\sigma_{\Re}$ is the strength associated with the relationship, and $k$ is the arity of the relationship type for the considered pair of names. Note that, for $SYN$ relationship, $k = 1$ in the thesaurus.

A presentation of the concept `Private Subject` according to these four different perspectives is shown in Fig. 3.

***Roles.*** The proposed structure of database ontology is intended to serve the following different purposes:

- Providing a semantic network search space for powerful mechanisms to locate the concept to which a given schema element refers and find other related concepts/elements in the ontology (network and taxonomic perspectives).
- Providing a reference basis for recognizing terminological relationships between names used in different database schemas (terminological perspective).
- Providing a support for mediator services for query formulation and processing, to correctly answer a query issued by a user, making retrieved data understandable by exploiting the ontology (frame perspective).

## 3. The proposed approach to ontology design

We take a discovery-based approach to ontology design, starting from the database conceptual schemas, or metadata, describing the database contents at the intensional level. This approach has been conceived and subsequently experimented in the framework of two research projects carried on in collaboration with the italian Information Systems Authority for the Public Administration (AIPA) [7, 4], to reduce manual classification activity in application domain analysis and organization. In these projects, an ontology is required to provide a unified view of the data manipulated by processes and/or stored in the databases of different information systems. The ontology will constitute the reference structure to understand and share the information spread in the different systems, to enhance information system cooperation. In this context, the following requirements hold and have an impact on the method to be defined for ontology design:

- *Availability of domain knowledge encoded in database schemas.* A repository of conceptual schemas is the starting point for constructing the ontology, coupled with knowledge held "a-priori" on the domain. This repository contains about 2500 Entity-Relationships data schemas related to the different Ministries of the Central Public Administration. Techniques are necessary to analyze the information encoded in the schemas (domain knowledge) and to support the extraction of general concepts, representative of different elements describing the same piece of information in different schemas.

- *Scalability of the approach.* It is important to develop scalable techniques, allowing for a systematic and computer-based analysis also with a large number of data schemas.

- *Composability/tailoring of the techniques.* Flexible analysis techniques are required, since the number and nature of schemas to be analyzed can vary in time and/or can not be known a priori. For example, if a set of conceptual schemas must be analyzed designed following methodological guidelines, the user can rely on meaningful name choices, and techniques for schema analysis based on names can be exploited. Consequently, an important requirement for the approach is that techniques to be applied are not fixed a priori, but can be selected and composed according to the characteristics of the schemas under analysis.

- *User interaction.* A completely automated approach is not feasible, since the problem presents typical requirements of schema analysis and view integration processes [3]. Consequently, interactive techniques are suggested to allow the user to validate intermediate results on the basis of his experience and knowledge, to come up with a coherent and consistent usage of the schema terminology within the ontology.

These requirements, which characterize our working environment in the project, are not peculiar of this project however. In fact, they can be applied in other database cooperation scenarios of inter-networked information sources (e.g., Web-based information systems, database federations, multidatabase systems). Such kind of scenarios are characterized by the presence of several, independently designed databases that require to share (part of) their data for cooperation. The possibility of extracting ontologies from database schemas is attractive since it allows the establishment of reference concepts for query processing by directly exploiting the information coded in the schemas exported by each database.

Based on these requirements, we developed a two-stage discovery process for the analysis of database schemas and the extraction of ontology concepts. The stages are the following:

- *Classification stage*, to build clusters of schema elements that are semantically similar in different schemas to be represented by means of a unique concept in the ontology.

- *Unification stage*, to extract ontology concepts from clusters of similar elements.

A comprehensive view of the discovery-based approach is shown in Fig. 4, where the following levels are identified from the bottom to the top: i) *extensional level*, concerning database instances; ii) *intensional level*, concerning database schemas; iii) *inter-schema knowledge level*, corresponding to clusters of semantically similar elements of the database schemas constructed by means of the similarity analysis and classification techniques; iv) *ontology knowledge level*, corresponding to concepts and inter-concept links of the ontology,

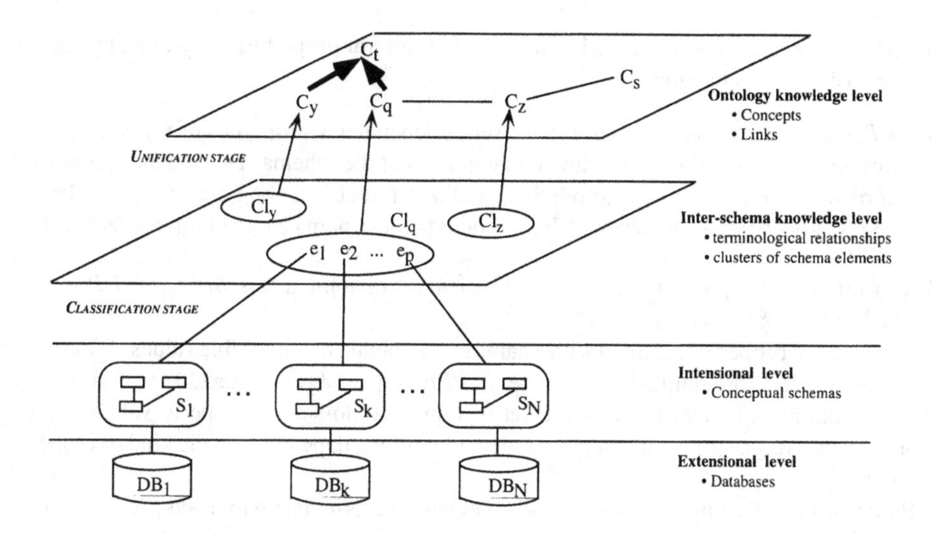


*Figure 4.* Levels of knowledge in the ontology

derived by means of the unification techniques.
The last two levels of knowledge are obtained as the result of the discovery process, and represent database schema information in an abstract, integrated, and unified way through the ontology concepts and links and the associated inter-schema knowledge.

### 3.1. *Reference data model*

The proposed approach for ontology design relies on a *reference data model*, introduced to reason in a formal way on the contents of the schemas to be analyzed. To avoid the definition of a further model, we adopt the model presented in [23]. It is based on the relational model augmented with basic object-oriented features. By adopting this model, we can uniformly analyze relational [2], entity-relationship [3], and object-oriented [9] source schemas.

The reference data model includes *relations* and *classes*. Relations contain tuples, while classes contain objects, which have a unique identifier. Classes have attributes and can belong to "is-a" hierarchies, with attribute inheritance. Moreover, in order to treat relations and classes uniformly, auxiliary relations are associated with classes and integrity constraints are defined as in [23]. In the following, we introduce a general notation for this model, which is based on the concept of *element*, to denote either a relation or a class in a source schema, and on the concept of *property* to denote an attribute of both relations and classes.

Let $S = \{S_1, S_2, \ldots, S_N\}$ be a collection of $N$ source schemas of heterogeneous data sources required to cooperate. A source schema is a collection of elements, $S_i = \{e_{1i}, e_{2i}, \ldots, e_{mi}\}$. A schema element $e_{ji} \in S_i$ is defined as a triple
$e_{ji} = \langle n(e_{ji}), SP(e_{ji}), DP(e_{ji})\rangle$, where:

- $n(e_{ji})$ is the name of the element, which is unique within the schema to which the element belongs.

- $SP(e_{ji}) = \{sp_1, sp_2, \ldots, sp_q\}$ is the set of structural properties of $e_{ji}$, i.e., properties describing $e_{ji}$'s features.
- $DP(e_{ji}) = \{dp_1, dp_2, \ldots, dp_r\}$ is the set of dependency properties of $e_{ji}$, i.e., properties describing relationships with other elements of the schema. Dependency properties correspond to foreign keys of relations and to references among classes. For a dependency property $dp_k$, we use $ref(dp_k)$ to denote the schema element referenced by $dp_k$.

The different sets of properties for a given element are disjoint, that is, $SP(e_{ji}) \cap DP(e_{ji}) = \emptyset$ and $P(e_{ji}) = SP(e_{ji}) \cup DP(e_{ji})$.

Each kind of property is defined with a name and a domain of admissible values. We denote by *PRE* the set of pre-defined domains (e.g., *PRE* = {`integer, smallint, decimal, float, char[n]`}), and by *REF* the set of reference domains. Property values can be atomic values (e.g., strings, integers) or object identifiers, depending on the kind of property domain.

Properties can be single-valued or multi-valued. We associate with each property a pair $(mc, MC)$, with $mc \leq MC$, to denote its minimum and maximum cardinality, respectively. Consequently, a property $p_k \in P(e_{ji})$ is defined as a triple $p_k = \langle n_{p_k}, d_{p_k}, (mc, MC)_{p_k} \rangle$, where:

i) $n_{p_k}$ is the property name, unique within $e_{ji}$;

ii) $d_{p_k}$ is the property domain, with $d_{p_k} \in PRE$ or $d_{p_k} \in REF$

iii) $(mc, MC)_{p_k}$ is the property cardinality, with $mc = MC = 1$ if $p_k$ is single-valued, and $MC = n$, with $n > 1$, if $p_k$ is multi-valued.

For a schema element, a subset of its properties, $K(e_{ji}) \subseteq P(e_{ji})$, constitutes its identifier or key. This means that different instances of $e_{ji}$ cannot have the same values for properties in $K(e_{ji})$.

## 4. The classification stage

In this section, we provide the theoretical foundations of the classification stage, in term of functions and properties, and the computer-based classification techniques developed in our projects.

### 4.1. *Theoretical foundations*

The classification stage requires two functions: a *clustering function*, called $GROUP()$, and a *similarity function*, called $SIMIL()$. The purpose of the clustering function is to group all elements that are semantically similar in the analyzed schemas into *clusters*. The similarity function for pairs of schema elements determines their level of semantic similarity in their respective schemas.

Let $E$ be the set of schema elements to be analyzed, that is, $E = \{e_i \mid e_i \in S_j, j = 1, \ldots, N\}$.

The $GROUP()$ function is defined as follows:

$$GROUP() : E \rightarrow 2^E$$

where $2^E$ is the powerset of $E$. $GROUP()$ starts from the set of schema elements to be analyzed and returns sets (i.e., clusters) of semantically related elements, on the basis of the $SIMIL()$ values for pairs of elements. Let $Cl_k \in 2^E$ be a cluster of semantically similar elements.

The following property holds for $GROUP()$:

($\mathbf{P_1}$) *Homogeneity.* The value of $SIMIL()$ between each possible pair of elements in a given cluster $Cl_k$ is always greater than the $SIMIL()$ value between an element outside $Cl_k$ and any element of $Cl_k$.
$e_h \notin Cl_k \Rightarrow SIMIL(e_i, e_j) \geq SIMIL(e_i, e_h)$, **forall** $Cl_k$, **forall** $e_i, e_j \in Cl_k$.

This property ensures that in a given cluster we can find the most similar elements among all possible elements of $E$.

The $SIMIL()$ function is defined as follows:

$$SIMIL() : E \times E \rightarrow [0, 1]$$

$SIMIL()$ is evaluated on schema elements with respect to *comparison features*. Different kinds of comparison features can be selected for schema elements (e.g., names of the elements, structural properties). Let us denote by $CF(e_i)$ the set of comparison features of a schema element $e_i$. Not all possible pairs of comparison features of two schema elements are relevant for the evaluation of $SIMIL()$, but only the pairs that have a *semantic correspondence*. Two comparison features have a semantic correspondence if they describe the same real-world information. Let $cf \in CF(e_i)$ be a comparison feature of $e_i$. We denote by $\sim$ the existence of a semantic correspondence between comparison features of different elements. Let $CF(e_i) \cap CF(e_j) = \{(cf, cf') \mid cf \in CF(e_i), cf' \in CF(e_j), cf \sim cf'\}$ be the set composed of the pairs of comparison features that have a correspondence in $e_i$ and $e_j$.

The following properties are defined for $SIMIL()$.

($\mathbf{P_2}$) *Nonnegativity.* The semantic similarity of two elements is nonnegative and is at most 1.
$\forall e_i, e_j \in E, SIMIL(e_i, e_j) \geq 0$ **and** $SIMIL(e_i, e_j) \leq 1$.

($\mathbf{P_3}$) *Null value.* $SIMIL()$ for two elements $e_i$ and $e_j$ is null if they do not have comparison features with semantic correspondence.
$CF(e_i) \cap CF(e_j) = \emptyset \Rightarrow SIMIL(e_i, e_j) = 0$.

($\mathbf{P_4}$) *Identity.* The comparison of an element with itself always returns the greatest semantic similarity value.
$SIMIL(e_i, e_i) = 1$.

($\mathbf{P_5}$) *Commutativity.* The semantic similarity of two elements is independent of their comparison order.
$SIMIL(e_i, e_j) = SIMIL(e_j, e_i)$

($\mathbf{P_6}$) *Monotonicity.* Adding comparison features with semantic correspondence to a pair of schema elements cannot decrease their semantic similarity.

$(CF(e_i) \cap CF(e_j)) \subset (CF'(e_i) \cap CF'(e_j)) \Rightarrow SIMIL_{CF}(e_i, e_j) \leq SIMIL_{CF'}(e_i, e_j)$, with $CF(e_i) \subset CF'(e_i)$ **and** $CF(e_j) \subset CF'(e_j)$[1].

**(P₇)** *Maximum value.* $SIMIL()$ has value 1 for two elements $e_i$ and $e_j$ if all features of $e_i$ have a semantic correspondence with features of $e_j$ and vice versa, that is, $\forall cf \in CF(e_i) \exists cf' \in CF(e_j), (cf, cf') \in (CF(e_i) \cap CF(e_j))$ **and** $\forall cf \in CF(e_j) \exists cf' \in CF(e_i), (cf, cf') \in (CF(e_i) \cap CF(e_j)) \Rightarrow SIMIL(e_i, e_j) = 1$.

Criteria for the establishment of semantic correspondences between comparison features depend on the kind of feature under consideration. For example, using element names as comparison features, semantic correspondences can be established using a criterion based on terminological relationships (e.g., synonymy). In next section, we will discuss criteria for the establishment of semantic correspondences between names and properties of schemas elements.

### 4.2. *Classification techniques*

In this section, we describe computer-based techniques for classification of schema elements.

To cluster semantically similar schema elements, we adopt classical clustering techniques of hierarchical type [10], used in Information Retrieval for document classification [30]. The general hierarchical clustering procedure is the following.

1. ***Hierarchical Clustering Procedure***:
2. /* **Input:** $K$ schema elements to be analyzed */
3. Compute $K \cdot (K-1)/2$ $SIMIL()$ coefficients;
4. Place each schema element into a cluster of its own;
5. *repeat*
6. Select the pair $Cl_j, Cl_h$ of clusters such that $M[j,h] = max_{s,t} M[s,t]$;
7. Form a new cluster by combining $Cl_j$ and $Cl_h$;
8. Update $M$ by deleting the rows and columns of $Cl_j$ and $Cl_h$;
9. Define a new row and column for the new cluster $Cl_{jh}$;
10. *until* rank of $M = 1$;
11. End pseudo-code.

As the result of clustering, a *similarity tree* is obtained, where several clusters, with an associated $SIMIL()$ value, can be identified. In the similarity tree, leaves are schema elements and other nodes are virtual schema elements which abstract the commonalities of their children elements[2] and an associated $SIMIL()$ value. The root represents the centroid of all classified elements, and its $SIMIL()$ value can be null, if no commonalities are identified among all analyzed schema elements. Several element clusters can be identified in a similarity tree, whose number of elements depends on the selected value of $SIMIL()$. In the following, we denote by $Cl_p^S$ a cluster in the similarity tree with its corresponding $SIMIL()$ value.

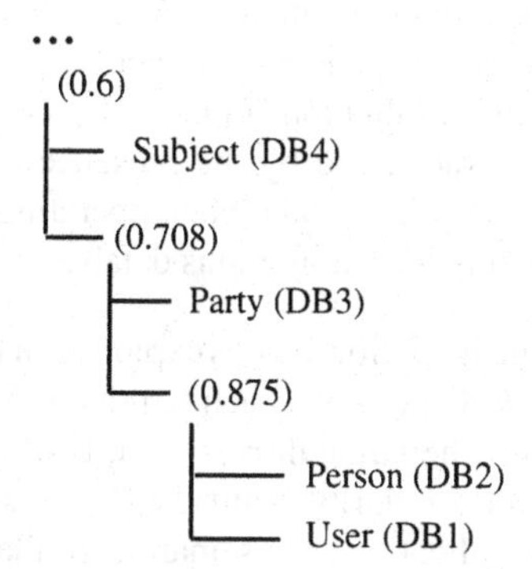


*Figure 5.* Schema element cluster for the `Private Subject` concept

As an example, in Fig. 5, we show the cluster associated with the concept `Private Subject` for the `Land Department` databases, characterized by a similarity value of 0.6.

Let us now come to the similarity techniques. Two different techniques have been developed for the evaluation of the $SIMIL()$ function:

- A *structure-based* technique, with which element comparison reaches the level of property domain, by considering compatibility of domains with respect to type and structure in different databases. We denote by $SIMIL_1()$ the semantic similarity value obtained by applying this technique.

- A *terminology-based* technique, with which element comparison is performed by exploiting terminological relationships between elements, by considering their kind and number of occurrences in the analyzed schemas. We denote by $SIMIL_2()$ the semantic similarity value obtained by applying this technique.

Motivations for developing two different similarity analysis techniques are related to the necessity of coping with conceptual schemas at different levels of abstraction and/or designed with more or less accuracy, as we will discuss in more detail subsequently.

Both techniques perform the analysis and comparison of schema elements with respect to the following features:

1. *Name* of schema elements. Names are generally considered the first, heuristic indicator of the semantic similarity of elements in different schemas.

2. *Structural properties* of schema elements. Schema elements are compared with respect to their structural properties, to conclude about their similarity on the basis also of their structure. In fact, element names alone are in general a partial indicator of semantic similarity, which can be complemented by the analysis of the structure of schema elements. In the literature, attributes have been considered an important comparison factor in schema analysis and integration (see for instance [22, 31]).

3. *Dependency properties* of schema elements. Analysis of the context of elements in the schemas represented by the dependency properties provides knowledge that is also useful for semantic similarity evaluation. In fact, elements having the same real world semantics are generally characterized by the presence of common elements in their contexts. Element contexts are important when operating in distributed environments with ontological requirements for autonomous databases.

The thesaurus of terminological relationships is exploited in both techniques. To make the numerical evaluation of $SIMIL()$ possible, each terminological relationship $\Re$ is properly strengthened in the thesaurus. The strength $\sigma_{\Re} \in (0,1]$ of a terminological relationship $\Re$ expresses its implication for similarity, with $\sigma_{SYN} \geq \sigma_{BT/NT}$. Different types of relationships have different implications for semantic similarity. In particular, we have $\sigma_{SYN} \geq \sigma_{BT} \geq \sigma_{RT}$. We assign the highest strength to the $SYN$ relationship, since synonymy indicates entity similarity more precisely than remaining terminological relationships. As for $BT/NT$ and $RT$ strengths, we consider the semantic similarity implication of schema links represented by these relationships. Motivations to set $\sigma_{BT} \geq \sigma_{RT}$ are related to the fact that "is-a" links express a higher semantic connection between entities than relationships, as discussed in [32]. In our experimentation, we used $\sigma_{SYN} = 1$, $\sigma_{BT} = \sigma_{NT} = 0.8$, and $\sigma_{RT} = 0.5$. In the following, when necessary, we use notation $\sigma_{ij_{\Re}}$ to denote the strength of the terminological relationship $\Re$ for entity names $n(e_i)$ and $n(e_j)$ in the thesaurus.

#### 4.2.1. *Structure-based technique ($SIMIL_1()$)*

This technique is based on the concept of *affinity*, which identifies elements with semantic similarity with respect to a given comparison feature. With this technique, the semantic similarity value, denoted by $SIMIL_1()$, is evaluated by considering:

- the name of the elements, using a *Name Affinity coefficient*;
- the properties of the elements, using a *Structural Affinity coefficient.*

***Name Affinity.*** Given two schema elements $e_{ji}$ and $e_{hk}$, their Name Affinity coefficient, denoted by $NA(e_{ji}, e_{hk})$, is the measure of the affinity of their names $n(e_{ji})$ and $n(e_{hk})$ in the thesaurus, computed using an affinity function $A()$ as reported in Table 1.

For any pairs of names, *NA*() $\in [0,1]$. $NA()$ is 1 if the names coincide, or is equal to the strength of the path $\rightarrow^m$ in the thesaurus originating the highest strength value, if this value exceeds a specified threshold $\alpha$. In this case, $NA()$ is proportional to the length of $\rightarrow^m$ and to the strength of the involved relationships. In remaining cases, $NA()$ is 0. Symbol $\sim$ is used to denote affinity between names. For example, $n(e_{ji}) \sim n(e_{hk})$ indicates that name of $e_{ji}$ and name of $e_{hk}$ have affinity.

***Structural affinity.*** The evaluation of structural affinity is based on the properties of schema elements. Semantic correspondences are established between properties of elements with NA() by analyzing their names and domains. First condition in the establishment of a semantic correspondence between two properties is name affinity, to find properties with the same meaning. Second condition in the establishment of a semantic correspondence between two properties is "domain compatibility", to test if their data value representations

*Table 1.* Affinity coefficients.
**Legend.**
$n \rightarrow^m n'$ denotes the shortest path of length $m$, with $m \geq 1$, between $n$ and $n'$ in the thesaurus.
$\sigma_{l_{\Re}}$ denotes the strength of $l^{th}$ terminological relationship in $n \rightarrow^m n'$.
$\alpha$ is an affinity threshold set to filter out names with high affinity values.
$\mid X \mid$ denotes the cardinality of set $X$.

| Coefficient | Value | Condition |
|---|---|---|
| | $1$ | if $n = n'$ |
| $A(n, n')$ | $0 \leq \sigma_{1_{\Re}} \cdot \sigma_{2_{\Re}} \cdot \ldots \cdot \sigma_{(m-1)_{\Re}} \leq 1$ | if $n \rightarrow^m n'$ |
| | $0$ | in all other cases |
| $NA(e_{ji}, e_{hk})$ | $A(n(e_{ji}), n(e_{hk}))$ | if $A(n(e_{ji}), n(e_{hk})) \geq \alpha$ |
| | $0$ | if $A(n(e_{ji}), n(e_{hk})) \leq \alpha$ |
| $SA(e_{ji}, e_{hk})$ | $\frac{2 \cdot \mid\{[p_l] \in P^E_{jh} \mid [p_l]^{wf}\}\mid}{\mid P_{jh} \mid}$ | in all cases |

match each other. Based on this, two kinds of semantic correspondences are introduced for the evaluation of structural affinity of schema elements:

- *weak correspondence*, denoted by $\leftrightarrow^*$, if two properties have name affinity;
- *strong correspondence*, denoted by $\leftrightarrow$, if two properties have both name affinity and domain compatibility.

Conditions to be checked for domain compatibility depend on the kind of domain. For example, compatibility of two pre-defined domains can be due to the internal representation of values. For instance, with reference to SQL domains, examples of basic-level compatibility relationships that hold for pre-defined domains are the following: `char`$[n_1] \Leftrightarrow$ `char`$[n_2]$, `smallint` $\Leftrightarrow$ `integer`, `integer` $\Leftrightarrow$ `float`, `decimal` $\Leftrightarrow$ `float`, `smallint` $\Leftrightarrow$ `float`. Moreover, a compatibility relationship holds between a domain and its restrictions (e.g., `integer` $\Leftrightarrow$ $[min..max]$). Two pre-defined domains not compatible at the basic-level (e.g., `integer` and `char[n]`) can still be compatible if an isomorphism can be established between their values, with respect to the meaning of the values for the properties they are associated with (semantic-level compatibility). In case of reference domains, compatibility is evaluated on the names of the referenced elements, by requiring that they coincide or are synonyms in the thesaurus. Let $P_{jh} = P(e_{ji}) \cup P(e_{hk})$ be the set of properties of both $e_{ji}$ and $e_{hk}$. $\leftrightarrow$ and $\leftrightarrow^*$ are binary, equivalence relations on $P_{jh}$'s properties. Consequently, properties of $P_{jh}$ are partitioned into equivalence classes. For any property $p_l$ belonging to $P_{jh}$, the equivalence class to which $p_l$ belongs is denoted by $[p_l]$ and contains all properties which have a semantic correspondence $\leftrightarrow^*$ or $\leftrightarrow$ with $p_l$, that is, $[p_l] = \{p_k \in P_{jh} \mid p_k \leftrightarrow^* p_l \vee p_k \leftrightarrow p_l\}$. Let $P^E_{jh} = \{[p_l] \mid p_l \in P_{jh}\}$ be the set of equivalence classes resulting from $P_{jh}$. For the evaluation of Structural Affinity, only the so-called "well-formed" equivalence classes are of interest among those in $P^E_{jh}$. An equivalence class $[p_l]$ is said to be well-formed, denoted by $[p_l]^{wf}$, if it contains at least one property of $e_{ji}$ and one property of $e_{hk}$. We are now ready to formally define the Structural Affinity coefficient.

The Structural Affinity coefficient of two schema elements $e_{ji}$ and $e_{hk}$, denoted by $SA(e_{ji}, e_{hk})$, measures the level of overlapping between their properties based on well-formed equivalence classes as shown in Table 1.

The Structural Affinity coefficient returns a value in the range $[0, 1]$. The value 0 indicates that no well-formed equivalence classes are defined for properties of $e_{ji}$ and $e_{hk}$ (i.e., no semantic correspondences can be established between properties of $e_{ji}$ and $e_{hk}$). The value 1 indicates that all equivalence classes are well-formed (i.e., each property of $e_{ji}$ has a semantic correspondence with at least one property of $e_{hk}$ and vice versa). Intermediate values of $SA()$ are proportional to the number of well-formed equivalence classes. In the evaluation of Structural Affinity, if the same property of one element has a semantic correspondence with more than one property of the other one, the analyst intervention is requested. The analyst can specify which correspondences have to be maintained and considered for the computation of the $SA()$ coefficient.

*Definition 1.* The Semantic Similarity value $SIMIL_1(e_{ji}, e_{hk})$ of two elements $e_{ji}$ and $e_{hk}$, is evaluated as the weighted sum of their Name and Structural Affinity coefficients as follows,

$$SIMIL_1(e_{ji}, e_{hk}) = \begin{cases} w_{NA} \cdot NA(e_{ji}, e_{hk}) + w_{SA} \cdot SA(e_{ji}, e_{hk}) & \text{if } NA(e_{ji}, e_{hk}) \neq 0 \\ 0 & \text{otherwise} \end{cases}$$

where weights $w_{NA}$ and $w_{SA}$, with $w_{NA}, w_{SA} \in [0, 1]$ and $w_{NA} + w_{SA} = 1$, are introduced to assess the relevance of each kind of affinity in computing $SIMIL_1()$ function.

The use of weights is motivated by the need of flexible comparison strategies. In general, both coefficients are useful to discover elements with affinity in different schemas. The implications of the two kinds of affinity can be defined by properly setting the corresponding weight in $SIMIL_1()$. We tested different values for these weights, and we found that an intermediate situation with $w_{NA}, w_{SA} = 0.5$ gives satisfactory results.

*4.2.2. Terminology-based technique ($SIMIL_2()$)* This technique is based on terminological relationships in the thesaurus. With this technique, the semantic similarity value, denoted by $SIMIL_2()$, is evaluated by considering:

- the name and properties of the elements, in form of terminological relationships stored in the thesaurus.

***Classification of terminological relationships.*** Given a pair of elements, they can be connected by means of several types of terminological relationships in the thesaurus. Both the type and the number of occurrences of a given type of relationship between a pair of names $n_i$ and $n(e_i)$ have implications for the evaluation of $SIMIL_2()$ for elements $e_i$ and $e_j$.

A first classification of relationships distinguishes *explicit* and *implicit* relationships. Explicit relationships, denoted by the symbol "$\Re$", are terminological relationships stored in the thesaurus. Implicit relationships, denoted by the symbol "$\Rightarrow$", can be derived from the

*Table 2.* Functions for relationship strengths derivation.
**Legend.**
$\tau : [0,1] \rightarrow [0,1]$.
$\tau' : [0,1] \times [0,1] \rightarrow [0,1]$.
$\tau'' : [0,1] \times [0,1] \rightarrow [0,1]$.

| Function | Value | Condition |
|---|---|---|
| $\tau(\sigma_{ij})$ | $\sigma_{ij}^{1/k}$ | strength for homogeneous multiple relationships |
| $\tau'(\sigma_{ij_{BT}}, \sigma_{ij_{RT}})$ | $(\sigma_{ij_{BT}} + \sigma_{ij_{RT}}) - (\sigma_{ij_{BT}} \cdot \sigma_{ij_{RT}})$ | strength of heterogeneous relationships |
| $\tau''(\sigma_{ih}, \sigma_{hj})$ | $(\sigma_{ih} \cdot \sigma_{hj})$ | strength for implicit relationships |

explicit ones through the existence of paths between them. We restrict implicit relationships to paths involving no more than two relationships of type $BT$ or $RT$, and a $SYN$ relationship. Explicit and implicit relationships can occur more than once between a given pair of names. Orthogonally to the previous classification, we distinguish *homogeneous multiple relationships* and *heterogeneous multiple relationships*. An explicit relationship is homogeneous multiple, denoted by the symbol "$\Re^k_{hom}$", if its arity $k > 1$. An implicit relationship is homogeneous multiple, denoted by "$\Rightarrow^k_{hom}$", if it involves explicit relationships $\Re$ of the same type and at least one of them is multiple. Explicit relationships are heterogeneous multiple, denoted by "$\Re^k_{het}$', if they are of different type for the same pair of names (i.e., $BT$ and $RT$). An implicit relationship is heterogeneous multiple, denoted by "$\Rightarrow^k_{het}$", if it involves explicit relationships which are heterogeneous multiple in turn.

To derive the strength of each type of relationship starting from the strength assigned to explicit relationships in the thesaurus, we introduce the functions shown in Table 2.

According to this technique, $SIMIL_2(e_{ji}, e_{hk})$ is evaluated as follows.

*Definition 2.* The Semantic Similarity value $SIMIL_2(e_{ji}, e_{hk})$ is evaluated as the measure of the (highest) strength of the relationships verified between their names $n(e_{ji})$ and $n(e_{hk})$ in the thesaurus as follows:

$$SIMIL_2(e_{ji}, e_{hk}) = \begin{cases} 1 & \text{if } n(e_{ji}) = n(e_{hk}) \\ \tau(\sigma_{ij}) & \text{if } \langle n(e_{ji}) \Re^k_{hom} n(e_{hk}) \rangle, \\ & k \geq 1 \\ \tau'(\tau(\sigma_{ij_{BT}}), \tau(\sigma_{ij_{RT}})) & \text{if } \langle n(e_{ji}) \Re^k_{het} n(e_{hk}) \rangle \\ \tau''(\tau(\sigma_{ih}), \tau(\sigma_{hj})) & \text{if } \langle n(e_{ji}) \Rightarrow^k_{hom} n(e_{hk}) \rangle, \\ & k \geq 1 \\ \tau''(\tau'(\tau(\sigma_{ih_{BT}}), \tau(\sigma_{ih_{RT}})), \tau(\sigma_{hj})) & \text{if } \langle n(e_{ji}) \Rightarrow^k_{het} n(e_{hk}) \rangle \wedge \\ & \wedge \langle n(e_{ji}) \Re^k_{het} n' \rangle \\ \tau''(\tau(\sigma_{ih}), \tau'(\tau(\sigma_{hj_{BT}}), \tau(\sigma_{hj_{RT}}))) & \text{if } \langle n(e_{ji}) \Rightarrow^k_{het} n' \rangle \wedge \\ & \wedge \langle n' \Re^k_{het} n(e_{hk}) \rangle \\ 0 & \text{otherwise} \end{cases}$$

$SIMIL_2()$ verifies the properties in that it returns a numerical value in the range $[0,1]$. In particular, it returns: 1 for elements having identical names, the strength of the relationship(s) holding between their names in the thesaurus obtained by properly combining

*Table 3.* Comparison of the similarity techniques

| CHARACTERISTIC | $SIMIL_1()$ | $SIMIL_2()$ |
|---|---|---|
| **Name and properties** | Yes | Yes |
| **Property domain** | Yes | No |
| **Suggested use** | Detailed schemas with rich semantic information | High-level schemas with summary information |
| **Cluster** | Fine-grained semantic similarity Clusters of highly homogeneous schema elements | Coarse-grained semantic similarity Clusters of semantically related schema elements |
| **Required manual activity in the unification stage** | Limited, possibly not required correspondences | Required, cluster elements must be inspected |

the $\tau$ functions, and 0 otherwise. For a given pair of names, if both explicit and implicit relationships are defined for them, explicit relationships take precedence over the implicit ones. Moreover, if more than one implicit relationship is defined for the considered pair of names, the one with the highest strength $\tau''$ is selected as the measure of semantic similarity.

### 4.3. *Considerations*

The different similarity techniques presented above can be applied to differently specialized application contexts, because they require different levels of information. The structure-based technique supports an in-depth analysis of similarity, requiring detailed schema descriptions, and provides automated support to concept unification. The terminology-based technique can be applied when high level schema descriptions are available and requires additional information to be manually provided to derive ontology concepts. In Table 3, the different techniques are compared according to their basic characteristics.

## 5. The unification stage

### 5.1. *Theoretical foundations*

The purpose of the unification function for ontology design is to derive representative concepts from clusters of semantically similar elements.

We call $UNIFY()$ the unification function, which is defined as follows:

$$UNIFY() : 2^E \rightarrow C$$

$UNIFY()$ starts from clusters of semantically related elements and returns concepts. Let $C_k$ be a concept of the ontology derived from a cluster $Cl_k$ of schema elements.

The following properties hold for $UNIFY()$:

($\mathbf{P_8}$) *Disjointness.* Disjoint clusters of schema elements are unified into distinct concepts of the ontology.

$C_k \neq C_q \Rightarrow Cl_k \cap Cl_q = \emptyset$ **forall** concepts $C_k$ and $C_q$ obtained from a cluster.

($\mathbf{P_9}$) *Property union.* Properties of a concept $C_k$ are the union of the properties of the elements in its corresponding cluster $Cl_k$.
$P(C_k) = \bigcup P(e_i)$ **forall** $e_i \in Cl_k$.

In particular, the union operation means that only one property is defined for $C_k$ representative of all properties that have a semantic correspondence in different elements of $Cl_k$.

($\mathbf{P_{10}}$) *Property intersection.* Featuring properties of a concept $C_k$ are the intersection of the properties of the elements in its corresponding cluster $Cl_k$.
$FP(C_k) = \bigcap P(e_i)$ **forall** $e_i \in Cl_k$[3].

### 5.2. *Unification techniques*

Ontology concepts are defined starting from *candidate clusters* of the similarity tree. Candidate clusters are defined as follows.

*Definition 3.* A candidate cluster, denoted by $\overline{Cl}_q$, is a cluster of the similarity tree characterized by a value of *SIMIL*() greater than or equal to a given threshold $\gamma$, that is,

$$\overline{Cl}_q = Cl_q^S \textbf{ such that } S \geq \gamma$$

Each cluster candidate for being unified into a concept is selected within the similarity tree by considering *SIMIL*() values therein contained. One can decide to automatically select as candidate clusters only the ones with very high values of *SIMIL*(), or, alternatively, the ones having a not null value of *SIMIL*(). The difference is in the number and nature of resulting concepts. In the first case, a higher number of concepts is defined unifying highly homogeneous elements. The possibility of re-organizing concepts into generalization hierarchies should be evaluated. In the second case, a lower number of concepts is defined, unifying more heterogeneous elements. In such a case, the need of generalization hierarchies in the ontology is reduced. An automatic criterion for selection of candidate clusters is not definable, in that it depends on the semantic similarity values in the tree. We found out that candidate clusters can be identified progressively, by starting from the ones with the highest values of *SIMIL*() (i.e., clusters at the bottom level of the tree) and by moving upwards in the tree, to include other elements until the affinity coefficient is judged significant.

Let $\overline{Cl}_q \in T$ be a candidate cluster within the similarity tree. Candidate clusters are the starting point for defining ontology concepts, through the unification of schema elements belonging to them ($UNIFY()$ function). Cluster shown in Fig. 5 is selected as candidate by setting $\gamma = 0.5$.

***Unification rules.*** Techniques for unification of elements in a candidate cluster are based on unification rules for the derivation of concept names and concept properties (considering also their domains and cardinality). Unification rules are reported in Table 4. According to rule ($\mathbf{UR_1}$), the name $\overline{n}$ unification of a pair of names with affinity $n_i \sim n_j$ can coincide with one of them or can be one of their hypernyms or synonyms in the thesaurus.

Let $p_t$ and $p_q$ be two properties with $p_t \leftrightarrow p_q$ or $p_t \leftrightarrow^* p_q$. We define the rules for unifying domains and cardinalities, respectively. According to rule ($\mathbf{UR_2}$), the domain $\bar{d}$ unification of two domains $d_{p_t}$ and $d_{p_q}$ is semi-automatically derived in presence of

*Table 4.* Unification rules.
**Legend.**
$n_h \in \mathrm{BT}(n_i) \cup \mathrm{BT}(n_j) \cup \mathrm{SYN}(n_i) \cup \mathrm{SYN}(n_j)$, where $\mathrm{BT}(n_k) = \{n_h \mid \langle n_h\ BT\ n_k \rangle\}$ is the set of hypernyms of $n_k$ and $\mathrm{SYN}(n_k) = \{n_h \mid \langle n_h\ SYN\ n_k \rangle\}$ is the set of synonyms of $n_k$ in the thesaurus.
$\Delta_{\mathrm{UR}_1}$ denotes unification by applying rule $(\mathbf{UR_1})$.

| Rule | Value | Condition |
|---|---|---|
| $(\mathbf{UR_1})$ | $n_i$ or $n_j$ or $n_h$ | if $n_i \sim n_j$ |
| $(\mathbf{UR_2})$ | $d'$ | if $(p_t, p_q \in SP()) \vee (p_t, p_q \in DP() \wedge d_{p_t}, d_{p_q} \in PRE) \wedge p_t \leftrightarrow p_q$ |
| | $n(ref(p_t))\ \Delta_{\mathrm{UR}_1}\ n(ref(p_q))$ | if $(p_t, p_q \in DP()) \wedge (d_{p_t}, d_{p_q} \in REF) \wedge p_t \leftrightarrow p_q$ |
| | $d_{p_t}$ | if $p_t \in SP() \wedge p_q \in DP() \wedge p_t \leftrightarrow p_q$ |
| | $d_{p_t}$ | if $(p_t, p_q \in DP()) \wedge (d_{p_t} \in PRE \wedge d_{p_q} \in REF) \wedge p_t \leftrightarrow p_q$ |
| | manually supplied | if $p_t \leftrightarrow^* p_q$ |
| | $\perp$ | in all remaining cases |
| $(\mathbf{UR_3})$ | $\overline{mc} = min\{mc_{p_t}, mc_{p_q}\}$ | always |
| | $\overline{MC} = max\{MC_{p_t}, MC_{p_q}\}$ | always |

strong correspondences. Different solutions are possible depending on the possible cases (see Table 4). In particular, if $p_t$ and $p_q$ are structural properties or dependency properties with pre-defined domains (i.e., foreign keys of relations), then $\bar{d}$ is defined as a domain $d'$ coinciding with the less restrictive domain between them. For example, if $d_{p_t} = \texttt{char}[n_1]$ and $d_{p_q} = \texttt{char}[n_2]$, we have $\bar{d} = \texttt{char}[n]$, with $n = max\{n_1, n_2\}$. As another example, if $d_{p_t} = \texttt{integer}$ and $d_{p_q} = \texttt{smallint}$, we have $\bar{d} = \texttt{integer}$.
If $p_t$ and $p_q$ are dependency properties with reference domains, the domain $\bar{d}$ is obtained by applying rule $(\mathbf{UR_1})$ to the names of the referenced elements. In case of a structural property and a dependency property, or two dependency properties with a pre-defined and a reference domain, $\bar{d}$ coincides with the pre-defined domain.

For properties with a weak correspondence, the corresponding unified domain is manually supplied. For example, if $d_{p_t} = \texttt{char}[n_1]$ and $d_{p_q} = \texttt{integer}$, the domain $\bar{d}$ is set equal to one of them only if an isomorphism can be established between the values of $d_{p_t}$ and $d_{p_q}$. Conversion functions are necessary to transform values of $d_{p_t}$ or $d_{p_q}$ according to $\bar{d}$.
If no unified domain can be specified, $\bar{d} = \perp$, meaning that the unification is not applicable.

According to rule ($\mathrm{UR}_3$), the cardinality $(\overline{mc}, \overline{MC})$ unification of two cardinalities $(mc, MC)_{p_t}$ and $(mc, MC)_{p_q}$ is defined as the less restrictive cardinality between the two.

***Unification of schema elements.*** In analogy with the view integration process, we adopt a binary strategy to derive ontology concepts from candidate clusters. We distinguish between "unification in the small" and "unification in the large" of schema elements. Unification in the small is the basic step to derive a concept from two cluster elements. Unification in the large iteratively applies unification in the small to derive a concept from clusters containing more than two schema elements.

The unification in the small of two elements $e_{ji}$ and $e_{hk} \in \overline{Cl}_q$ into a concept $C_{jh}$ consists of the following steps:

**Derivation of the name of $C_{jh}$.** Name $n(C_{jh})$ of $C_{jh}$ is obtained by applying $(\mathbf{UR_1})$ to the names of $e_{ji}$ and $e_{hk}$, $n(C_{jh}) = n(e_{ji})\ \Delta_{\mathrm{UR}_1}\ n(e_{hk})$.

**Derivation of properties of $C_{jh}$.** For each equivalence class $[p_l] \in P_q^E$ such that exist $p_t$ and $p_q$ belonging to $[p_l]$ with $p_t \in P(e_{ji})$ and $p_q \in P(e_{hk})$ (or vice versa), a unique concept property $\bar{p} = \langle \bar{n}_{\bar{p}}, \bar{d}_{\bar{p}}, (\overline{mc}, \overline{MC})_{\bar{p}} \rangle$ is defined as follows,

1. $$\bar{n}_{\bar{p}} = \begin{cases} n_{p_t} \triangle_{\mathrm{UR}_1} n_{p_q} & \text{if } (p_t, p_q \in \mathit{SP}()) \vee (p_t, p_q \in \mathit{DP}()) \\ n_{p_t} \triangle_{\mathrm{UR}_1} n(\mathit{ref}(p_q)) & \text{if } p_t \in \mathit{SP}() \wedge p_q \in \mathit{DP}() \end{cases}$$

2. $$\bar{d}_{\bar{p}} = d_{p_t} \triangle_{\mathrm{UR}_2} d_{p_q}$$

3. $$(\overline{mc}, \overline{MC})_{\bar{p}} = (mc, MC)_{p_t} \triangle_{\mathrm{UR}_3} (mc, MC)_{p_q}.$$

Each derived concept property $\bar{p}$ is classified as follows:

1. $\bar{p} \in \mathit{SP}(C_{jh})$ if $p_t$ and $p_q$ are both structural properties or if one of them is a structural property and the other one is a dependency property. Properties obtained in this way become properties for concept $C_{jh}$.
2. $\bar{p} \in \mathit{DP}(C_{jh})$ if $p_t$ and $p_q$ are dependency properties. Such properties are used to establish links among concepts, as discussed below.

Orthogonally to previous classifications, if $[p_l]$ is well-formed, $\bar{p}$ is marked as featuring property.

Unification in the large of candidate clusters containing more than two elements is performed by unifying in the small pairs of elements at a time. Results of the unification in the small are accumulated into intermediate concepts which gradually evolve towards the final concept $C_q$, representative of all elements included in $Cl_q$. The order for element comparison is bottom-up, starting from the pair with the highest $SIMIL()$ value in $Cl_q$.

### 5.3. *Establishment of links between concepts*

Once concepts have been defined through the unification techniques, they are analyzed to check their mutual consistency and to define links for them. Links among concepts are defined by analyzing the properties of the concepts and of the elements in their corresponding clusters:

- *kind-of* links can be defined by analyzing properties of and/or clusters associated with concepts. Two cases can occur. i) A *kind-of* link is defined between two existing concepts $C_q$ and $C_k$. If two existing concepts have a number of common properties, they can be related by means of a *kind-of* link, to highlight the subsumption relationship between them (e.g., $C_q$ *kind-of* $C_k$). For the establishment of the link, only $BT$ relationships hold between the elements in the cluster associated with $C_k$ and the elements in the cluster associated with $C_q$. For example, with reference to Fig. 1, the *kind-of* links between `Private Subject` and `Legal Entity` and between `Private Subject` and `Individual` have been defined in this way. ii) Definition of a new concept with *kind-of* links with existing concepts. Also in this case, common properties are identified for existing concepts and a new concept is introduced to abstract such commonalities by means of a subsumption relationship. For example, with reference to Fig. 1, since concepts `Public Subject` and `Private Subject` have common properties denoting names and codes, a new concept `Subject` is introduced with properties `Subject_Code` and `Subject_Name`.

- *association* links are defined by analyzing dependency properties of defined concepts. Two cases can occur. i) A featuring dependency property has been defined for a concept $C_q$ (i.e., properties with a semantic correspondence exist in all schema elements in $\overline{Cl_q}$) and a concept $C_z$ has been extracted from elements referenced by dependency properties of schema elements in the cluster. In this case, a link is defined between $C_q$ and $C_z$, capturing the association between the underlying schema elements at the concept level. ii) A dependency property not featuring has been abstracted for a concept $C_q$ (i.e., properties with a semantic correspondence exist in a number of schema elements in $\overline{Cl_q}$), and a concept $C_z$ has been defined representative of schema elements referenced by $Cl_q$ elements. In this case, the decision of defining a link between $C_q$ and $C_z$ is left to the user.

Restructuring of ontology concepts can be necessary after establishing links. For example, if an *association* link has been established between two concepts $C_q$ and $C_z$, then the involved dependency properties of $C_q$ and $C_z$ need to be revised and possibly removed. This to maintain concepts consistent each other and express the association between them only by means of links.

## 6. Usages of the database ontology

In this section, we describe the usages of the database ontology according to the different roles outlined in Section 2.

***Browsing/querying the search space.*** The browsing mode is useful to support the user in exploring the information space to discover concepts semantically related to the information managed in a given database. In the browsing mode, once the user locates a concept $C_k$ of interest, possibly with an associated cluster $Cl_k$, taxonomic and network perspectives can be invoked to explore the concept space and find other concepts related to $C_k$. For instance, the taxonomic perspective can be invoked to display the immediate parents and children of a given concept. A set of pre-defined functions, listed in Table 5, are available to display information stored in the concept frame, and to present it according to the different perspectives.

When a user is interested in finding remote information similar to the information managed locally, he can formulate a query to locate the appropriate concept in the ontology. Given a schema element $e_i$ of interest for the user, the ontology can be queried with the following query format:
*RETRIEVE* $e_i$
[*WHERE*
  [*PROPERTY* $\langle sp_1, \ldots, sp_t \rangle$]]

*Table 5.* Functions for ontology browsing

| Function | Description |
|---|---|
| *Display-Properties()* | Returns all properties of $C_k$ |
| *Display-FProperties()* | Returns all featuring properties of $C_k$ |
| *DisplayKindOf()* | Returns all superconcepts of $C_k$ |
| *DisplaySub()* | Returns all subconcepts of $C_k$ |
| *DisplayAssociation()* | Returns all concepts related to $C_k$ |
| *DisplayInstances()* | Returns all schema elements in cluster $Cl_k$ |

[*ASSOCIATION* $\langle n_1, \ldots, n_k \rangle$]]

where $e_i$ is the target element, $\langle sp_1, \ldots, sp_t \rangle$ are property names and $\langle n_1, \ldots, n_k \rangle$ names of related elements that the target element must possess. Notation "[ ]" indicates optional clauses.

Evaluation of this query involves identifying the concept $C_k$ of which $e_i$ is instance, and retrieving its associated cluster $Cl_k$. As the result of the query, schema elements (different from $e_i$) belonging to $Cl_k$ are proposed to the user, possibly filtered according to the conditions specified in the *WHERE* clause of the query. For example, suppose that a user operating on entity `Subject` in database $DB_4$ is interested in finding information on other possible types of subjects in Land databases. The user can formulate a *RETRIEVE* query specifying element `Subject` as the target. As a result of the query, schema elements belonging to the cluster of Fig. 5 are presented to the user.

***Terminology mediation.*** In this mode, ontology concepts associated with element clusters allow the mediation between different terminologies adopted in different databases to denote the same piece of information. According to the taxonomic and terminological perspective, given a schema element it is possible to retrieve its associated cluster and analyze the terminological relationships holding between cluster elements in the thesaurus. For example, it is possible to determine the shortest path between two names in the thesaurus, and analyze the involved terminological relationships. This way, the user gets the different names adopted in the different databases to denote a given concept.

## 7. Scalability and maintenance issues

In this section, we discuss issues related to scalability of the ontology construction process and to the maintenance of the ontology, once it has been created.

### *7.1. Scalability*

The proposed techniques for ontology construction can be differently applied, giving origin to different processes, according to the requirements of the environment where the ontology is to be used. The following processes are possible for establishing a database ontology: i) *One-step process*: all the conceptual schemas are analyzed at the same time to produce the ontology concepts by applying the proposed techniques; ii) *Incremental process*: ontology concepts are incrementally defined, by considering one schema at a time, and by properly assimilating schema elements with already defined concepts; iii) *Mixed process*: the one-step process is applied to a bulk of schemas to produce an initial set of ontology concepts, which is incrementally enriched/extended by assimilating new schemas, following the incremental process. The different kind of processes are suitable in different integration scenarios.

- *Historical/legacy databases*. The ontology is a tool to systematize and organize the knowledge to facilitate the consultation and interfacing of existing databases. In this scenario, databases are available a priori and, consequently, the number and typology of data schemas can be considered quite static. The one-step process is applied to analyze the available data schemas, possibly obtained from a reverse engineering activity.
- *Internet databases*. The ontology is a tool to mediate among the different information contexts of the database sites, to facilitate the cooperation over the Internet. In this scenario, a high variety of schemas is to be considered and, consequently, we have a large and dynamic information space. The incremental process is suitable for ontology construction, to cope with scalability issues typical of such kind of scenario.
- *Intranet/Extranet databases*. The ontology is a tool to organize knowledge on a number of databases, to share the available information and facilitate the acquisition of new, external information. In this scenario, an initial set of databases is available and databases can be incrementally and dynamically considered and represented in the ontology. The mixed process is suitable to progressively extend the concepts actually represented in the ontology, starting from an initial set of concepts.

### 7.2. *Ontology maintenance and interoperation*

The maintenance process deals with the assimilation of a new database schema into the existing ontology concepts. This problem can be addressed by using the proposed techniques and by exploiting additional domain knowledge provided together with the data schema(s) to be assimilated.

When a new schema is proposed for assimilation, the local analyst is required to specify a set of terminological relationships (i.e., $SYN$, $BT/NT$, $RT$) that hold for element and property names in the domain. This activity can be simplified by referring to existing domain-specific dictionaries or to lexical system (see for example WordNet [13, 29]), to automatically retrieve and propose to the local analyst information about synonyms, hypernyms and hyponyms for the schema to be assimilated. The assimilation of new schema elements requires the restructuring of existing ontology concepts, and is performed by applying the analysis techniques. The thesaurus is updated with new terminological relationships of schema elements to be assimilated. Then, similarity coefficients $S()$ are evaluated between new elements and the existing ontology concepts, to determine how to assimilate new schema elements. To fasten the process, it is possible to base the similarity analysis only on the featuring properties of concepts, which provide the essential information for characterizing concepts in the ontology. Depending on the results of the similarity analysis, two assimilation alternatives are possible: i) restructuring: a new schema element becomes an instance of the most similar existing ontology concept, if a similar concept exists in the ontology; ii) enrichment: a new concept is defined to represent the new schema element when no similar concepts exist in the ontology. A similarity threshold is used to filter out the most similar ontology concept(s).

Ontology interoperation deals with the problem of assimilating different ontologies developed using our approach. To this end, we can consider ontologies as schemas in the approach, and apply the proposed techniques as well.

## 8. Experimentation of the approach

Our techniques have been experimented on a set of ER conceptual schemas of the Public Administration information systems. Examples derived from these experimentations are presented in this section. The classification and unification techniques have been implemented in the ARTEMIS supporting tool environment. ARTEMIS is developed in Java and provides functionalities for similarity-based analysis and clustering of source schemas, and for cluster unification into ontology concepts. It provides also some basic functionalities for a semi-automatic construction of the thesaurus, by analyzing the source schemas with parsing tools. A Web-based interface has also been developed to access the ontology according to the different perspectives.

### *8.1. Application of the mining techniques using the structure-based similarity*

In this section, we present the results of an experimentation on the Entity-Relationship schemas of databases of the Department of Incomes of the Ministry of Treasury of the italian Central Public Administration.

In particular, we considered the `Tributary Register` ($DB_1$) database, storing data on the tax status of the taxpayers, the `VAT Office DB` ($DB_2$) database, storing data on the formal checks performed by the responsible offices on the income-tax declarations presented by the taxpayers, and the `Direct Taxes` ($DB_3$) database, storing data on income-tax declarations, on payments, and on the taxpayers. These relational databases pertain to different organization units of the Ministry, contain interrelated data regarding income-tax declarations and taxpayers, and have been maintained separated for a long time. Now such databases are required to cooperate and share part of their data, due to a new law recently established for improving the transparency of the procedures and unify the tax payment procedures. The ER schemas of $DB_1$, $DB_2$, and $DB_3$ used for the analysis are reported in Fig. 6.

These schemas have been analyzed according to the structure-based technique, since the detailed schemas are available to be unified in view of query processing. $SIMIL_2()$ coefficients between all pairs of schema entities have been evaluated, and the clustering procedure has been applied to group entities with affinity. For the sake of simplicity, we select a portion of the whole affinity tree, which is shown in Fig. 7(b). This portion is related to the candidate cluster $\overline{Cl_1}$ containing schema entities describing the different taxpayers in $DB_1$, $DB_2$, and $DB_3$. The affinity value of $\overline{Cl_1}$ is 0.6, meaning that it contains homogeneous entities. In Fig. 7(a) the concept `Taxpayer` obtained by unifying

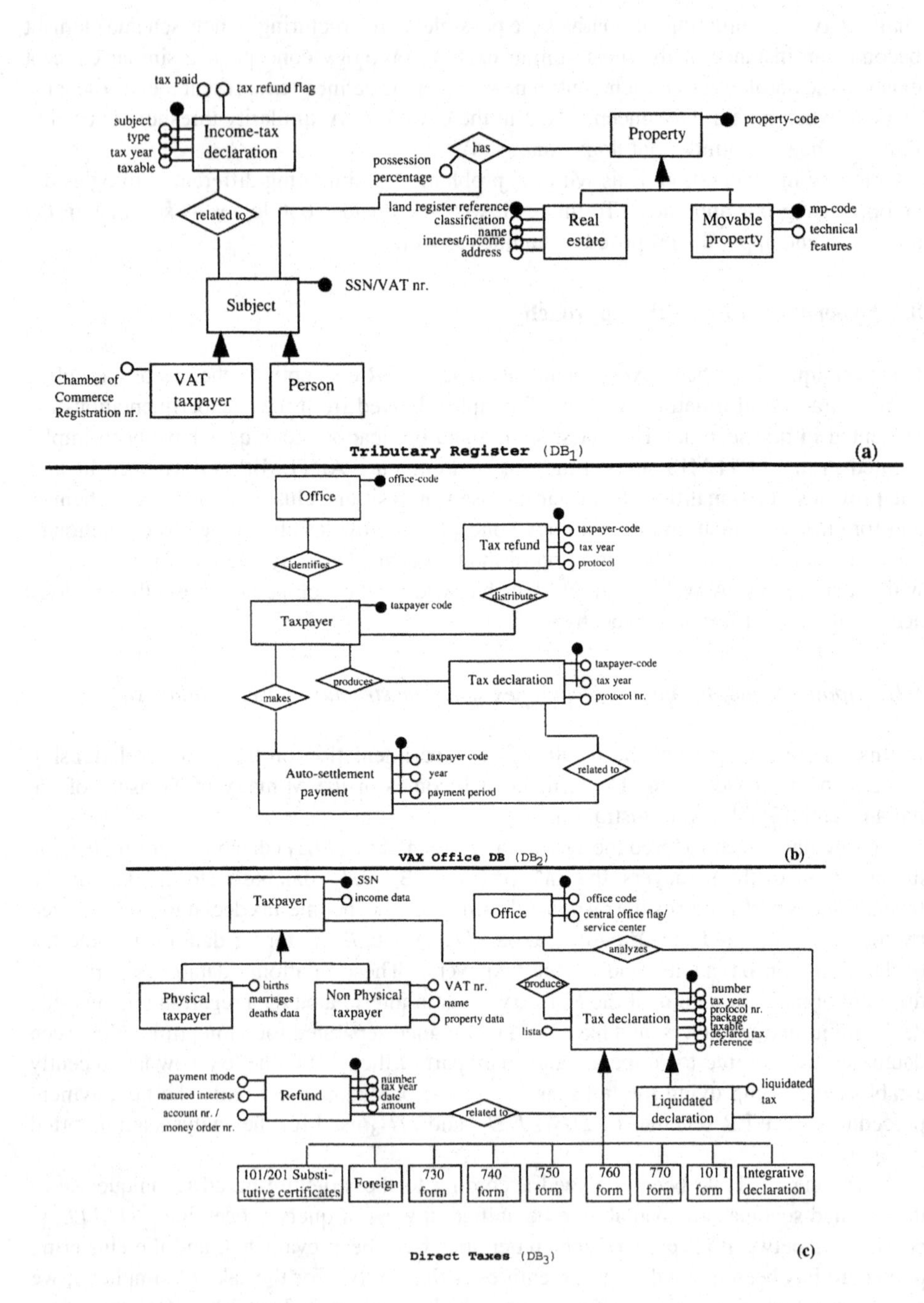


*Figure 6.* Conceptual schema of databases $DB_1$, $DB_2$, and $DB_3$

| **Concept Frame** | |
|---|---|
| *Name* | Taxpayer |
| *Properties* | SSN, Registration nr., Income data, VAT nr., Name, Births Marriages Deaths data, Property data |
| *Featuring Properties* | SSN, VAT nr., Income data. |
| *Kind-of* | { } |
| *Subconcepts* | { } |
| *Association* | {Office, TaxRefund, TaxDeclaration}. |
| *Instances* | {DB1.Subject, DB2.Taxpayer, DB1.Person, DB1.VATTaxpayer, DB3.PhysicalTaxpayer, DB3.NonPhysicalTaxpayer} |

**(a)**

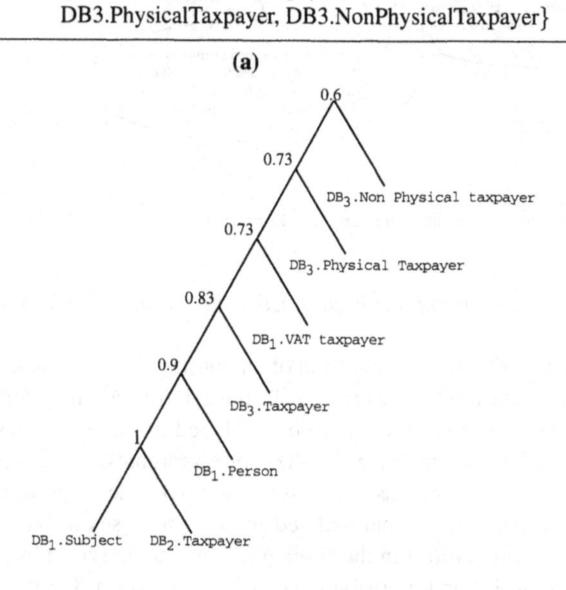


**(b)**

*Figure 7.* `Taxpayer` concept frame (a) and associated candidate cluster (b)

$\overline{Cl}_1$'s entities is shown. As the result of the unification process, the following concepts are defined:

- `Taxpayer` representing information related to taxpayers;
- `Tax Refund` representing information related to refunds;
- `Tax Declaration` representing information related to income-tax declarations presented by the taxpayers;
- `Office` representing information related to the offices that check income-tax declarations.

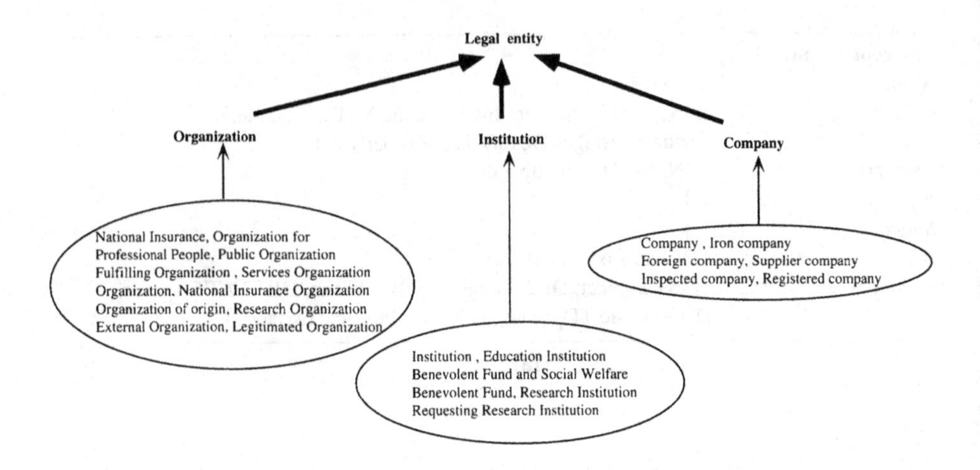


*Figure 8.* A sample of ontology for the `Ministry of Labour`

## *8.2. Application of the mining techniques using the terminology-based similarity*

In this section, we describe the construction of an ontology for 149 ER conceptual schemas of the Public Administration `Ministry of Labour` information systems, containing 542 entities. In this case, the ER schemas to be analyzed are at a high level of abstraction, describing entities, relationships and generalization hierarchies. Attributes are not specified, since the purpose of such schemas is to give a summary description of the information (i.e., non-structured data types) manipulated by the processes in terms of typology and relationships. In general, entities in these schemas are characterized by long names, which can provide also a description for attributes (which are missing). For these reasons, schema analysis has been performed using the terminology-based technique. Clustering of schema entities has been performed using two different hierarchical clustering procedures, that are the complete link and the single link procedures [30]. First we defined a concept in correspondence of candidate clusters in the complete-link tree, then we organized concept links based on information provided by clusters of the single-link similarity tree.

Entity clusters obtained with the complete link technique are a good basis to define ontology concepts. In fact, in the complete link tree we can find several small candidate clusters characterized by high similarity values, which contain names related to very homogeneous entities. In our experimentation, we obtained an average value of $SIMIL()$ for cluster of 0.762 in the complete-link tree. Clusters characterized by high similarity values (e.g., $> 0.7$) have been selected for concept definition, for a total number of 90 clusters with an average number of 4 entities per cluster.

An ontology concept defined for such kind of clusters represents a generalization of entities contained in the cluster. Example of concepts derived from the complete-link tree are `Organization`, `Institution`, and `Company`, which are shown Fig. 8 together with the entities forming the corresponding cluster. To assign a suitable name to the corresponding concept, we applied the name unification rule. The ARTEMIS tool implements this rule and tries to automatically assign a name to a given concept, based on terminological relationships defined in the thesaurus for entity names belonging to the analyzed candidate cluster, and on the frequency of hypernym terms in the cluster. For example, with reference to Fig. 8, a concept with name `Institution` has been defined because `Institution` is a hypernym of the entity names in the cluster. Analogously, we defined concept `Organization` as representative of all associated entities. In our experimentation, the tool was able to find a concept name in an automated way for 69 clusters (corresponding to the 76.67%); of these only in 6 cases, a manual revision was necessary. In addition, in 2 cases, the same name was selected for different concepts, which has not been interpreted as a fault, but instead as an indicator of a semantic relationship between the entities in the clusters. Finally, only in 4 cases, the names automatically assigned to concepts based on the unification rule were meaningless, and we noted that this occurred in presence of very long entity names, with several prepositions and adverbs. The user can interactively revise ambiguous cases and can assign a name by hand to concepts representative of clusters for which a name was not automatically assigned.

To identify higher-level concepts and establish links for concept composition, we cannot rely on properties and analyze, for example, commonalities to be abstracted into a higher-level concept, through a *kind-of* link. Instead, we can rely on information provided by entity clusters in the single link tree. Due to the way this technique operates, in the single link tree, we can find large clusters where it is possible to recognize clusters previously identified in the complete link tree. A non-null similarity value for these large clusters can be used as a heuristic indicator of the existence of a semantic relationship between corresponding concepts already extracted from complete-link clusters. A more abstract concept can be defined in the ontology to capture this semantic relationship between already defined concepts. This requires a highly interactive process since an automated support is not feasible in this case, and represents the most difficult part of the whole process. In general, the most frequently occurring links established between identified concepts were *kind-of* and *association*. *Kind-of* between concepts links are recognized mainly based on $BT$ relationships between concept names, and by studying the entities in the involved clusters. For example, let us consider in Fig. 9, a cluster ($Cl_1$) obtained with the single link technique. $Cl_1$ contains all entities appearing in clusters associated with `Institution` and `Organization` concepts, respectively, together with two additional entities (underlined in the figure) describing companies (which give origin to the `Company` concept of Fig. 8). Since the similarity value characterizing $Cl_1$ is $0.8$, we recognize that concepts `Institution`, `Organization`, and `Company` have a semantic relationship. This information is used for defining a superconcept `Legal Entity` as a generalization of them. A *kind-of* link is defined between `Legal Entity` and each underlying concept. The concept hierarchy resulting from this process is shown in Fig. 8.

The abstraction process has been applied until we found complete-link clusters having a non-null similarity value in the single link tree. Starting from the 90 concepts previously obtained, we derived 15 higher-level concepts for them. We found that, in general, at most three-levels of *kind-of* links are sufficient to capture the relationships holding between concepts.

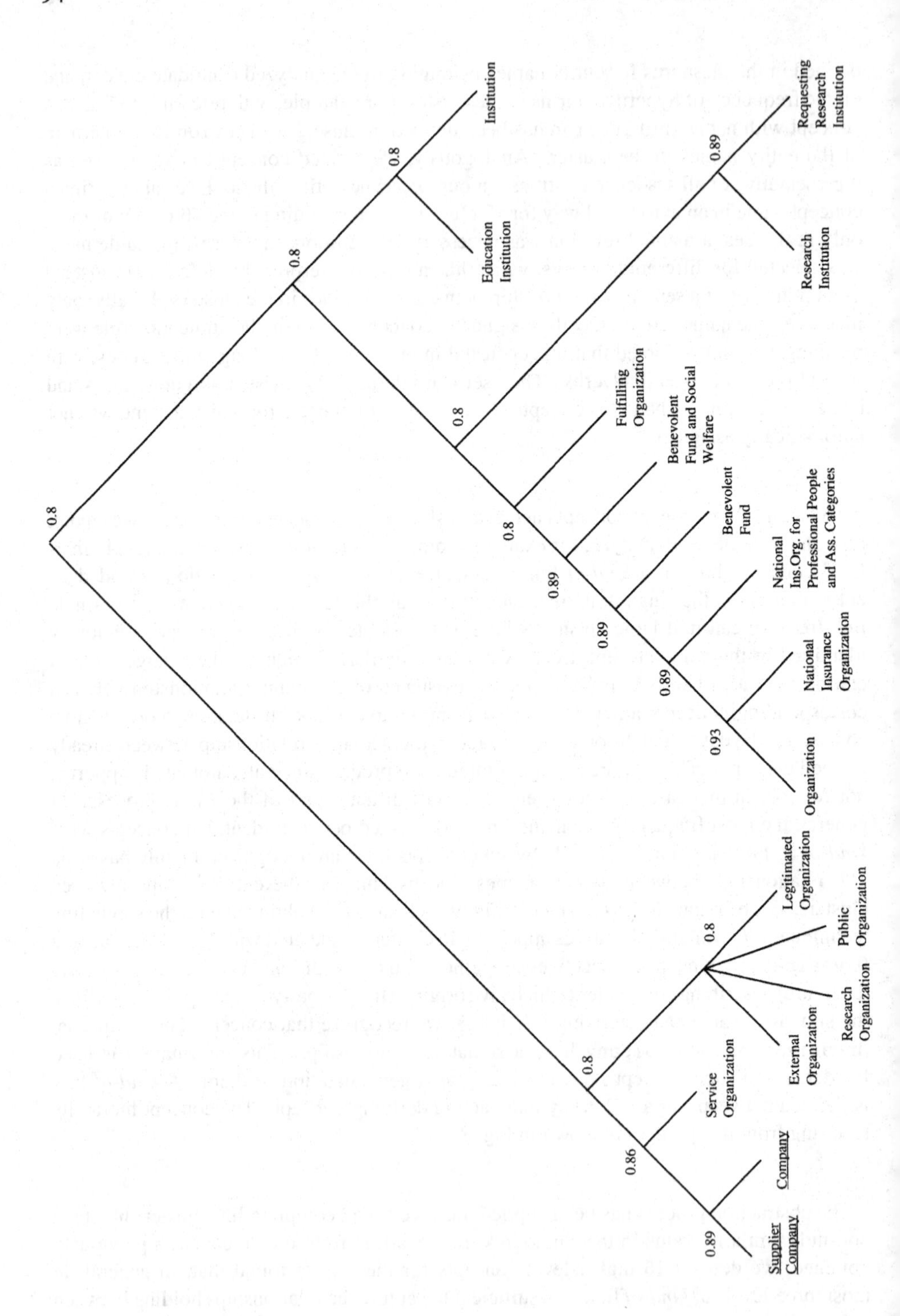


*Figure 9.* An example of entity cluster ($Cl_1$)

## 9. Related work

Work related to database ontology design ranges from information integration, to ontology design and software agents systems areas.

***Information integration.*** The problem of integrating information from heterogeneous sources to provide uniform access is widely studied in the literature. Several approaches have been proposed for the extraction and integration of heterogeneous information sources [1, 6, 5, 19, 26, 24]. Information integration usually relies on mediators [34]. In a mediator-based integration architecture, inter-schema knowledge about multiple data sources is properly encoded in the mediator providing services to identify and resolve conflicting situations thus enhancing interoperability and cooperation [34]. For example, the TSIMMIS architecture [12] relies on mediator components to combine information from heterogeneous sources, and on wrapper/translator components to convert data and queries into a common model. Here the emphasis is on definition of mediator rules and on languages for declarative specification of mediators, while techniques for the identification of semantically related elements in different sources are not considered. In [6], an approach is presented based on classification of names of the schema elements of source databases into a Summary Schema Model (SSM), which plays the role of a database ontology. SSM is based on an existing concept taxonomy and thesaurus for the underlying domain and schema elements/properties are (manually) mapped to the the most suitable taxonomy concept. Hypernymy and synonymy relationships are thus established between schema names that are used for query processing. A knowledge-based approach to build an integrated schema in a federation of relational databases is presented in [5]. With this approach, relations, attributes, and integrity constraints in sources schemas are translated into a terminology. Then, different terminologies are integrated to obtain the federated terminology which provides unified, ontological information about data sources. In [26], interactive techniques are presented to identify, in existing concept hierarchies, the right location where to place new schema elements to be assimilated. The assimilation process can be performed manually by a sharing advisor with required knowledge, or with the help of sharing heuristics based on the notion of "distinguishing capability" of properties with respect to a concept. In [19], distributed heterogeneous databases are clustered around a set of global concepts, describing at an abstracted level the information stored in different source bases. Global concepts provide an ontology to describe a cross-database application domain and facilitates access to the information services within this domain. Another approach based on metadata is taken in the OBSERVER system, developed to provide semantically rich queries on distributed information repositories where different vocabularies are used [27]. The system exploits metadata and domain ontologies associated with the different repositories together with inter-ontology relationships to handle vocabulary heterogeneity in query processing.

***Ontology design and agent systems.*** Work in this area is generally related to the design of formal ontologies and their role in supporting knowledge sharing among software entities [17]. The concept of formal ontology and some basic principles of ontology design are illustrated in [16], where a classification of ontologies according to their level of detail and their level of dependence on a particular task or point of view is given. A set of criteria to guide the development of ontologies as a way of specifying content-specific agreements for knowledge sharing and reuse is described in [14], and a discussion about the application of such criteria to case studies is provided. Issues related to the design of an ontology for natural language processing are described in [28], where the adopted structure and its usages are detailed.

Software agent systems play an essential role in modern information systems, based on Internet and on the Web [21]. Such systems provide intelligent capabilities for information brokering on distributed sources and for organizing discovered information to facilitate search activities. An ontology for agents provides a shared virtual world giving them a useful domain of discourse on which to base the interactions [18]. For example, the Ontolingua project at Stanford [15] provides integrated tools for constructing domain-specific ontologies represented in the Knowledge Exchange Format, that can be translated into application-oriented languages. An open-format language to represent ontological information on Web contents has been developed, called Meta Content Format [25]. Information in Web sites can then be organized according to this language, and viewers for exploring the resulting spaces (called Xspaces) are available for browsers.

## 10. Concluding remarks

In this paper, we have presented a discovery-based approach for the establishment of a database ontology starting from existing database schemas. Concepts in the ontology are presented according to four different perspectives to serve different purposes, such as browsing/querying the ontology search space and mediating the different terminologies adopted in the databases. In particular, we have proposed techniques for the *classification stage*, to build clusters of schema elements that are semantically similar in different schemas to be represented by means of a unique concept in the ontology, and for the *unification stage*, to extract ontology concepts from clusters of similar elements.

Future research work will be devoted to the extension of the approach and of the tool with facilities to support query processing and optimization against distributed databases, to determine which databases contain the data relevant to answer a query issued by a user by exploiting the ontology.

## Acknowledgments

We would like to thank Dr. S. De Capitani Di Vimercati for her collaboration on initial joint work on affinity-based analysis.

## Notes

1. Notation $SIMIL_{CF}(e_i, e_j)$ is used to indicate that $SIMIL()$ is evaluated with respect to features in $CF$.
2. Virtual schema elements are called "centroids" in the literature [10].
3. $\bigcap P(e_i)$ denotes the set of properties that are common (i.e., have a semantic correspondence) to all the elements of $Cl_k$.

## References

1. Y. Arens, C.Y. Chee, C.N. Hsu, C.A. Knoblock, "Retrieving and Integrating Data from Multiple Information Sources," Int. Journal of Intelligent and Cooperative Information Systems, vol. 2, no. 2, pp. 127–158, 1993.
2. P. Atzeni, V. De Antonellis, Relational Database Theory, The Benjamin/Cummings Publishing Company, 1993.
3. C. Batini, M. Lenzerini, S.B. Navathe, "A Comprehensive Analysis of Methodologies for Database Schema Integration," ACM Computing Surveys, vol. 18, no. 4, pp. 322–364, 1986.
4. C. Batini, S. Castano, V. De Antonellis, M.G. Fugini, B. Pernici, "Analysis of an Inventory of Information Systems in the Public Administration," Requirements Engineering Journal, vol. 1, no. 1, Springer, pp. 47–62, 1996.
5. J.M. Blanco, A. Illarramendi, A. Goni, "Building a Federated Relational Database System: An Approach Using a Knowledge-Based System," Int. Journal of Intelligent and Cooperative Information Systems, vol. 3, no. 4, pp. 415–455, 1994.
6. M.W. Bright, A.R. Hurson, S. Pakzad, "Automated Resolution of Semantic Heterogeneity in Multidatabases," ACM Transactions on Database Systems, vol. 19, no. 2, pp. 212–253, June 1994.
7. S. Castano, V. De Antonellis, M.G. Fugini, B. Pernici, "Conceptual Schema Analysis: Techniques and Applications," ACM Transactions on Database Systems, (to appear).
8. S. Castano, V. De Antonellis, "Semantic Dictionary Design for Database Interoperability," in Proc. of ICDE'97, 13th IEEE Conf. on Data Engineering, Birmingham, 1997, pp. 43–54.
9. R. Cattell (ed.), The Object Database Standard: ODMG-93, Morgan Kaufmann, 1996.
10. B. Everitt, Cluster Analysis, Heinemann Educational Books Ltd, Social Science Research Council, 1974.
11. N.V. Findler, (Ed.), Associative Networks, Academic Press, 1979.
12. H. Garcia-Molina, et al., "The TSIMMIS Approach to Mediation: Data Models and Languages," in Proc. of the NGITS workshop, 1995 (available at ftp://db.stanford.edu/pub/garcia/1995/tsimmis-models-languages.ps).
13. J. Gilarranz J. Gonzalo, F. Verdejo, "Using the EuroWordNet Multilingual Semantic Database," in Proc. of AAAI-96 Spring Symposium Cross-Language Text and Speech Retrieval, 1996.
14. T.R. Gruber, "Towards Principles for the Design of Ontologies Used for Knowledge Sharing," Int. Journal of Human and Computer Studies, vol. 43, Nos.5/6, pp. 907–928, 1995.
15. T.R. Gruber, "Ontolingua: A Mechanism to Support Portable Ontologies," Tech. Rep. KSL 91-66, Stanford University, Knowledge System Laboratory, March 1992.
16. N. Guarino, "Semantic Matching: Formal Ontological Distinctions for Information Organization, Extraction, and Integration," in Information Extraction - A Multidisciplinary Approach to an Emerging Information Technology, LNAI no. 1299, pp. 139–170, 1997.
17. N. Guarino, R. Poli, (eds.), Formal Ontology in Conceptual Analysis and Knowledge Representation, Special Issue of the Int. Journal of Human and Computer Studies, vol. 43, Nos.5/6, Academic Press, 1995.
18. M.N. Huhns, M.P. Singh, "Ontologies for Agents," IEEE Internet Computing, vol. 1, no. 6, pp. 81–83, 1997.
19. M.A. Jeusfeld, M. Papazoglou, "Information Brokering," in [20].
20. B. Kramer, M. Papazoglou, H.W. Schmidt, (eds.), Information Systems Interoperability, RSP Press, John Wiley, 1998.
21. "Internet-Based Agents," Special Issue of IEEE Internet Computing, vol. 1, no. 4, July/August 1997.
22. J.A. Larson, S.B. Navathe, R. Elmasri, "A Theory of Attribute Equivalence in Databases with Application to Schema Integration," IEEE Transactions on Software Engineering, vol. 15, no. 4, pp. 449–463, 1989.
23. A.Y. Levy, A. Rajaraman, J.J. Ordille, "Querying Heterogeneous Information Sources Using Source Descriptions," in Proc. of VLDB'96, the 22th Int. Conf. on Very Large Databases, Mumbai (Bombay), 1996.
24. A.Y. Levy, D. Srivastava, T. Kirk, "Data Model and Query Evaluation in Global Information Systems," Int. Journal of Intelligent Information Systems, vol. 5, pp. 121–143, 1995.
25. Documentation available at *mcf.research.apple.com/*.
26. D. McLeod, A. Si, "The Design and Experimental Evaluation of an Information Discovery Mechanism for Networks of Autonomous Database Systems," in Proc. of ICDE'95, 11th Conf. on Data Engineering, Taiwan, 1995, pp. 15–24.
27. E. Mena, V. Kashyap, A. Sheth, A. Illarramendi, "OBSERVER: An Approach for Query Processing in Global Information Systems based on Interoperation across Pre-existing Ontologies," in Proc. of First IFCIS International Conference on Cooperative Information Systems (CoopIS'96), Brussels (Belgium), , June 1996, pp. 14–25.

28. "Mikrokosmos Ontology," Documentation available at *http://crl.nmsu.edu/research/Projects/mikro/htmls/ontology-htmls/onto.index.html*, 1996.
29. A.G. Miller, "WordNet: a lexical database for English," Communications of the ACM, vol. 38, no. 11, pp. 39–41, 1995.
30. G. Salton, Automatic Text Processing - The Transformation, Analysis and Retrieval of Information by Computer, Addison-Wesley, 1989.
31. A.P. Sheth, S.K. Gala, S.B. Navathe, "On Automatic Reasoning For Schema Integration," Int. Journal of Intelligent and Cooperative Information Systems, vol. 2, no. 1, pp. 23–50, 1993.
32. T.J. Teorey, G. Wei, D. L. Bolton, Koenig, J.A., "ER Model Clustering as an Aid for User Communication and Documentation in Database Design," Communications of the ACM, vol. 3, no. 8, 1989.
33. "Guidelines for the Construction and Development of Monoligual Thesauri," UNI ISO Report N.2788, 1993.
34. G. Wiederhold, "Mediators in the Architecture of Future Information Systems," IEEE Computer, vol. 25, pp. 38–49, 1992.

Distributed and Parallel Databases 7, 99–121 (1999)


# Load Balancing for Parallel Query Execution on NUMA Multiprocessors*

LUC BOUGANIM luc.bouganim@inria.fr
DANIELA FLORESCU daniela.florescu@inria.fr
PATRICK VALDURIEZ patrick.valduriez@inria.fr
*INRIA Rocquencourt, France*

*Received ; Revised June 9, 1997; Accepted August 1, 1997*

**Recommended by:** Tamer Ozsu

**Abstract.** To scale up to high-end configurations, shared-memory multiprocessors are evolving towards Non Uniform Memory Access (NUMA) architectures. In this paper, we address the central problem of load balancing during parallel query execution in NUMA multiprocessors. We first show that an execution model for NUMA should not use data partitioning (as shared-nothing systems do) but should strive to exploit efficient shared-memory strategies like Synchronous Pipelining (SP). However, SP has problems in NUMA, especially with skewed data. Thus, we propose a new execution strategy which solves these problems. The basic idea is to allow partial materialization of intermediate results and to make them progressivly public, i.e., able to be processed by any processor, as needed to avoid processor idle times. Hence, we call this strategy Progressive Sharing (PS). We conducted a performance comparison using an implementation of SP and PS on a 72-processor KSR1 computer, with many queries and large relations. With no skew, SP and PS have both linear speed-up. However, the impact of skew is very severe on SP performance while it is insignificant on PS. Finally, we show that, in NUMA, PS can also be beneficial in executing several pipeline chains concurrently.

**Keywords:** parallel databases, query execution, load balancing, NUMA, synchronous pipeline, execution engines

## 1. Introduction

Commercial database systems implemented on shared-memory multiprocessors, such as Sequent, Sun, Bull's Escala, are enjoying a fast growing success. There are several reasons for this [45]. First, like almost all parallel database systems, they are used primarily for decision support applications, (e.g., data warehouse) a strong market which is now doubling every year. Second, shared-memory provides a uniform programming model which eases porting of database systems and simplifies database tuning. Third, it provides the best performance/price ratio for a restricted number of processors (e.g., up to 20) [3].

Unlike shared-nothing [12], shared-memory does not scale up to high-end configurations (with hundreds of processors and disks). To overcome this limitation, shared-memory multiprocessors are evolving towards Non Uniform Memory Access (NUMA) architectures.

*This work has been done in the context of Dyade, a joint R&D venture between Bull and INRIA.

The objective is to provide a shared-memory programming model and all its benefits, in a scalable parallel architecture.

Two classes of NUMA architecture have emerged: Cache Coherent NUMA machines (CC-NUMA) [1, 16, 26, 28, 29], which statically divide the main memory among the nodes of the system, and Cache Only Memory Architectures (COMA) [14, 18], which convert the per node memory into a large cache of the shared address space. When a processor accesses a data item which is not locally cached, the item is shipped transparently from the remote memory to the local memory. Because shared-memory and cache coherency are supported by hardware, remote memory access is very efficient, only several times (typically four times) the cost of local access.

NUMA is now based on international standards and off-the-shelf components. For instance, the Data General nuSMP machine and the Sequent NUMA-Q 2000 [31] using the ANSI/IEEE Standard Scalable Coherent Interface (SCI) [23] to interconnect multiple Intel Standard High Volume (SHV) server nodes. Each SHV node consists of 4 Pentium Pro processors, up to 4 GB of memory and dual peer PCI/IO subsystems [10, 24]. Other examples of NUMA computers are Kendal Square Research's KSR1 and Convex's SPP1200 which can scale up to hundreds of processors.

The "strong" argument for NUMA is that it does not require any rewriting of application software. However, some rewriting is necessary in the operating system and in the database engine. In response to the nuSMP announcement from Data General, SCO has provided a NUMA version of Unix called Gemini [9], Oracle has modified its kernel [8] in order to optimize the use of 64 GB of main memory allowed by NUMA multiprocessors.

In this paper, we consider the parallel execution of complex queries in NUMA Multiprocessors. We are interested in finding an execution model well suited for NUMA which provides a balanced parallel execution. There are two dimensions for parallelizing complex queries: intraoperator parallelism (by executing each operator in parallel) and interoperator pipelined or independent parallelism (by executing several operators of the query in parallel). The objective of parallel query execution is to reduce query response time by balancing the query load among multiple processors. Poor load balancing occurs when some processors are overloaded while some others remain idle. Load balancing strategies have been proposed on either shared-nothing [2, 5, 11, 15, 25, 33, 38, 40, 47], shared-disk [22, 30, 32] or shared-memory [6, 21, 35, 41].

In shared-nothing, the use of a nonpartitioned execution model, i.e., where each processor potentially accesses all the data, is inefficient because of intensive remote data access. Thus, parallelism is obtained through data partitioning, i.e., relations are physically partitioned during query processing using a partitioning function like hashing. Then, each processor accesses only a subset of the data, thus reducing interference and increasing the locality of reference. However, a partitioned execution model has three main drawbacks: (i) overhead of data redistribution for complex queries, (ii) processor synchronization, (iii) difficult load balancing which requires much tuning.

One of the key advantages of shared-memory over shared-nothing is that execution models based on partitioning [17] or not [21, 32, 36] can be used. The use of nonpartitioned techniques eases load balancing and tuning. Moreover, there is no redistribution. However, it can lead to high interference and poor locality of reference. Shekita and Young [41] analytically compared the two approaches in a shared-memory context. It is concluded that, if cache effects are ignored, the two approaches have similar behavior.

A very efficient execution strategy for shared-memory is *Synchronous Pipelining* (SP) [21, 37, 41]. It has three main advantages. First, it requires very little processor synchronization during execution. Second, it does not materialize intermediate results, which incurs little memory consumption. Third, unlike shared-nothing approaches, it does not suffer from load balancing problems such as cost model errors, pipeline delay and discretization errors [49].

NUMA also allows using either model. However, the heterogeneous structure of the memory may impact the choice of one model. In this paper, we first show that an execution model for NUMA should not use data partitioning but should strive to exploit efficient shared-memory strategies like Synchronous Pipelining (SP). However, considering NUMA has two consequences which can worsen the impact of skewed data distributions [48] on load balancing. First, the global memory is potentially very large, and makes it possible for the optimizer to consider execution plans with long pipeline chains. Second, the number of processors is potentially large. We show that these two factors have a negative impact on SP in case of skew.

We propose a new execution strategy which solves the inherent problems of SP, which are magnified in NUMA. The basic idea is to allow partial materialization of intermediate results and make them progressivly *public*, i.e., able to be processed by any processor, as needed to avoid processor idle times. Hence, we call this strategy *Progressive Sharing* (PS). It yields excellent load balancing, even with high skew. In addition, PS can be beneficial in executing several pipeline chains concurrently. To validate PS and study its performance, we have implemented SP and PS on a 72-processor KSR1 computer which is a COMA multiprocessor.[1]

The paper is organized as follows. Section 2 presents the parallel execution plans, which are the input for the execution model. Section 3 discusses the relevance of shared-memory and shared-nothing execution models for NUMA. Section 4 details the SP strategy and discusses its problems in NUMA, in particular, with data skew. Section 5 describes our parallel execution model for NUMA. Section 6 describes our implementation on the KSR1 computer and gives a performance comparison of SP and PS. Section 7 concludes.

## 2. Definitions

Parallel execution plans are the input for the parallel execution model. A *parallel execution plan* consists of an operator tree with operator scheduling. Different shapes can be considered: left-deep, right-deep, segmented right-deep, or bushy. Bushy trees are the most appealing because they offer the best opportunities to minimize the size of intermediate results [41] and to exploit all kinds of parallelism [27].

The *operator tree* results from the "macroexpansion" of the query tree [19]. Nodes represent atomic operators that implement relational algebra and edges represent dataflow. In order to exhibit pipelined parallelism, two kinds of edges are distinguished: blocking

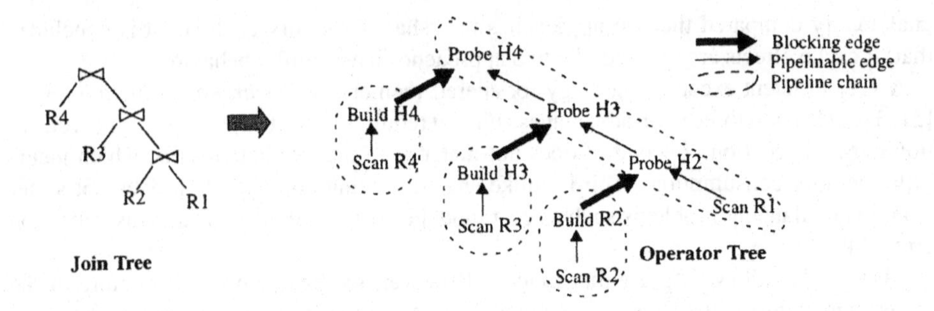


*Figure 1.* A query tree and the corresponding operator tree.

and pipelinable. A blocking edge indicates that the data is entirely produced before it can be consumed. Thus, an operator with a blocking input must wait for the entire operand to be materialized before it can start. A pipelinable edge indicates that data can be consumed "one-tuple-at-a-time". To simplify the presentation, we consider an operator tree that uses only hash join[2] [39, 46]. In this case, three atomic operators are needed: scan to read each base relation, build and probe. The build operator is used to produce a hash table with tuples from the inner relation, thus producing a blocking output. Then, tuples from the outer relation are probed with the hash table. Probe produces a pipelinable output, i.e., the result tuples.

An operator tree can be decomposed as a set of maximum pipeline chains, i.e., chains with highest numbers of pipelined operators, which can be entirely executed in memory. These pipeline chains are called fragments [41] or tasks [21]. Figure 1 shows a right-deep tree involving four relations and the corresponding parallel execution plan. Reading of relations R2, R3 and R4 as well as creation of the corresponding hash tables H2, H3 and H4 can be done in parallel. The execution of the last pipeline chain probing the hash tables is started only when H2, H3 and H4 have been built.

Assuming NUMA impacts the parallelization decisions made by the optimizer [43] since the available global memory is supposed to be large. Thus, with complex queries, we can expect that the best execution plans produced by the optimizer will often be bushy trees with long pipeline chains (at the extreme, only one pipeline chain) because they avoid materialization of intermediate results and provide good opportunities for inter- and intraoperator parallelism.

## 3. Execution models relevant for NUMA

In this section, we expose the two basic ways to process a multi-join query on a multiprocessor: (i) partitioned execution model with real pipeline, well suited for shared-nothing; and (ii) nonpartitioned execution model with implicit pipeline (synchronous pipeline), well suited for shared-memory. Then we present some experimental results from a previous study which help us selecting the best execution model for NUMA multiprocessors.

### 3.1. *Partitioned execution model*

In a shared-nothing architecture, a partitioned execution model is used in order to avoid intensive communication between processors. In such model, the execution of an algebra operator is split in suboperators, each one applied to a subset of the data. For example, the result of $R$ join $S$ can be computed as the union of the join of $R_i$ and $S_i$, if $R_i$ and $S_i$ were obtained by a partitioning function like hashing on the join attribute.

The problem of such approach is that each join operand must be redistributed on the join attribute, using the same partitioning function, before processing the join. This has three main drawbacks:

- The communication implied by the redistribution phase itself is very costly (however unavoidable in shared-nothing architecture).
- The redistribution phase implies a lot of synchronization between producers and consumers.
- Even with a perfect partitioning function, skewed data distributions [48] may induce uneven partitions. These uneven partitions may destroy the *locality of reference* obtained by the partitioning (to avoid unbalanced execution, the data will be dynamically redistributed).

### 3.2. *Synchronous pipeline strategy*

SP has proven to yield excellent load balancing in shared-memory [21, 37, 41]. Each processor is multiplexed between I/O and CPU threads and participates in every operator of a pipeline chain. I/O threads are used to read the base relations into buffers. Each CPU thread reads tuples from the buffers and applies successively each atomic operator of the pipeline chain using procedure calls. SP is, in fact, a simple parallelization of the monoprocessor synchronous pipeline strategy.

To illustrate this strategy, we describe below the algorithm of operator ProbeH2 (see figure 1):

```
1. ProbeH2(t_R1: Tuple(R1), H2: HashTable(R2))
2.     foreach tuple t_H2 in H2 matching with t_R1
3.         if pred(t_R1,t_H2) then ProbeH3([t_R1,t_H2], H3)
```

A procedure call to ProbeH2 is made for each tuple $t_{R1}$ that satisfies the Scan predicate. For each tuple produced by probing tuple $t_{R1}$ with the hash table H2, a procedure call is made to ProbeH3, and so on until producing the last result tuple of the pipeline chain.

Therefore, with synchronous pipeline, there is no synchronization between processors. In fact, the producer of a tuple is also its consumer (the tuple is the argument of the procedure call). However, during the join, each processor potentially accesses all the data involved in the join (and not a subset of the data as in a partitioned execution model).

### 3.3. Previous study

In [7], we have proposed an execution model, based on partitioning, called *Dynamic Processing* (DP), for a hierarchical architecture (i.e., a shared-nothing system whose nodes are shared-memory multiprocessors). In DP, the query work is decomposed in self-contained units of sequential processing, each of which can be carried out by any processor. Intuitively, a processor can migrate horizontally and vertically along the query work. The main advantage is to minimize the communication overhead of internode load balancing by maximizing intra- and interoperator load balancing within shared-memory nodes. Experimental comparison between DP and a classic static load balancing technique have shown performance gains between 14 and 39%.

In this study, we also compare the performance of DP and SP on a shared-memory machine. For this purpose, we had to simulate shared-memory on the KSR1. All data accesses were artificially made in the local memory, in order to avoid the effect of NUMA (remote memory access). The experiments have shown that, in a shared-memory multiprocessor, the performance of DP is close to that of SP (see figure 2(a)), which confirmed the analysis in [41].

As a starting point of the work herein described, we have modified our implementation on the KSR1 computer in order to take into account the NUMA properties of the KSR1, by making remote memory access for reading or writing tuples. To assess the relevance of a partitioned execution model for NUMA, we made measurements with the NUMA version of SP and DP. The same measurements as in [7] have shown a performance difference of the order of 35% in favor of SP (see figure 2(b)).[3]

The performance degradation of DP stems from intensive data redistribution (all relations), which implies interference between processors and remote data writing (much more costly than remote data reading during the probe phase of the synchronous pipeline strategy).

To summarize, a partitioned execution model is well suited for shared-nothing or hierarchical architectures. However, the use of a nonpartitioned execution model like SP seems more appropriate for NUMA.

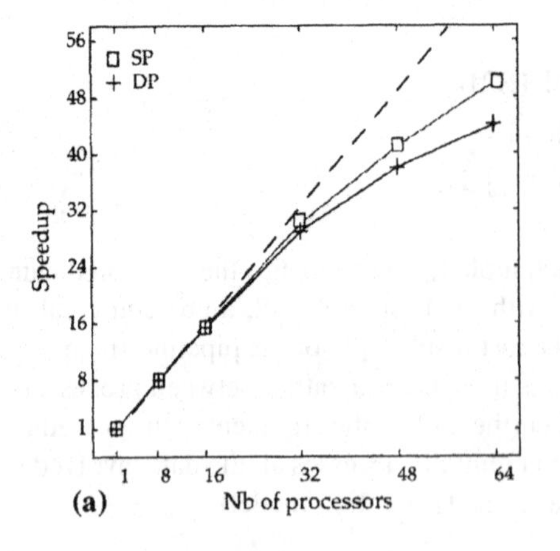


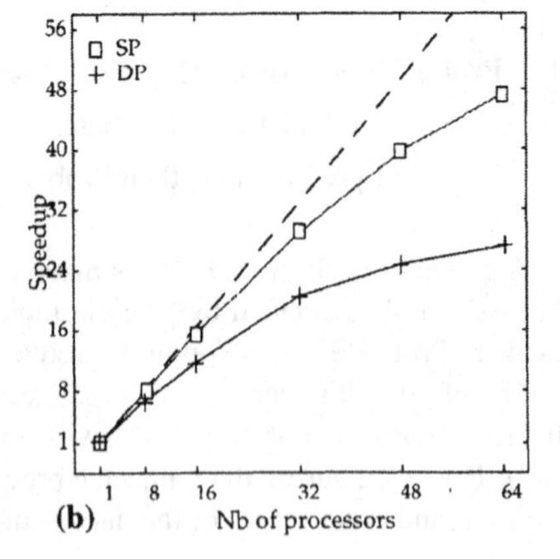


*Figure 2.* Speed-up of SP and DP: (a) on shared-memory, (b) on NUMA.

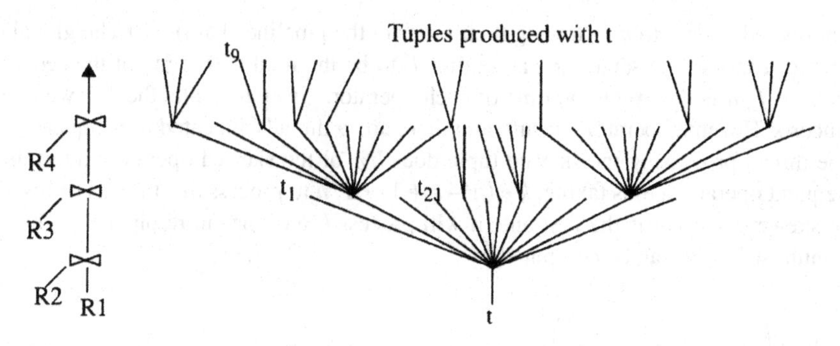


*Figure 3.* Processing of one tuple of R1.

## 4. Synchronous pipelining and data skew

Skewed (i.e., nonuniform) data distributions are quite frequent in practice and can hurt load balancing. The effects of skew on parallel execution are discussed in [48] in a shared-nothing context. The taxonomy of [48] does not directly apply to execution models which do not use data partitioning, as is the case for SP. As an evidence, *redistribution skew* does not hurt SP.

Figure 3 illustrates the processing of one tuple along the probe chain. The tuples produced by a tuple t of the base relation R1 form a virtual tree. Two observations can be made. First, SP does depth-first processing of this tree (for instance, t9 is produced before t21). At any time, the tuples being processed are referenced in the stacks of procedure calls. Second, all the tuples in the tree rooted at t are produced and processed by a single thread. On this simple example, we can indentify two kinds of skew that do hurt SP.

- **High selectivity skew** appears on a select operator (if any) at the beginning of the pipeline chain, if the result reduces to a small number of tuples, less than the number of threads. Since each tuple produced by the select operator is entirely processed (across the entire pipeline) by a single thread, this can lead to poor load balancing. An extreme case is when a single tuple is initially selected and the entire load generated is done by a single thread (while all the other threads are idle).
- **Product skew** appears on a join operator, when there are high variations in the numbers of matching tuples of the inner relation for the tuples of the outer relation. This is rare for joins on a key attribute, but quite frequent for inequi-joins or joins on non-key attributes.

These two kinds of skew lead to high differences in tuple processing time. Moreover, consuming base relations one-tuple-at-a-time can yield high interference overhead [6, 20] and this is generally avoided by having each thread consuming several tuples in batch mode. Given the fact that each batch is entirely processed by one thread, this can worsen the impact of skew.

To evaluate the negative effects of skew on a parallel execution in NUMA, we use a simple analytical model based on the following assumptions. (i) Only one operator of the pipeline chain, at the $r$th rank among $n$ operators, has skew (we consider that the operators are numbered from 1 to $n$ following their order in the pipeline chain). (ii) The global cost of each operator is the same, i.e., assuming $T$ to be the total CPU time of the sequential execution, $T/n$ is the execution time of each operator. (iii) One tuple, the "skewed" tuple produces $k\%$ of that operator's result, and there are $p$ threads allocated to the query.

The thread processing the skewed tuple does $k\%$ of the skewed operator and of all the subsequent operators, thus taking, $k * (n - r + 1) * \mathrm{T}/n$ to process this tuple. For instance, if the skewed operator is the first one, it will process $k\%$ of the entire pipeline. Thus, the maximum speed-up can be computed by:

$$\min\left(p, \frac{n}{k * (n - r + 1)}\right). \tag{1}$$

Figure 4 shows the speed-ups obtained versus $k$ for different ranks $r$ from one graph to the other. The results illustrate that even a small (but realistic) skew factor can have a very negative impact on the performance of SP.

Based on this simple model, we can observe that the speed-up degradation in case of skew depends on: (i) the skew factor $k$, (ii) the position $r$ of the skewed operator in the pipeline chain and (iii) the number of threads $p$. The speed-up gets worse as the skewed operator reaches the beginning of the chain. Furthermore, the maximum speed-up is bound by a factor independent on the number of processors. Therefore, the loss of potential gain increases with the number of processors.

Although it does not appear on our analytical model, the length of the pipeline chain also impacts load balancing in case of skew. When several operators are skewed, the negative effects can be, in the worst case, exponential in the length of the pipeline chain. A final consideration is the impact of batch size (the granule of parallelism) on load balancing. It seems obvious that load unbalancing, i.e., variations in batch processing time, increases with the batch size [20].

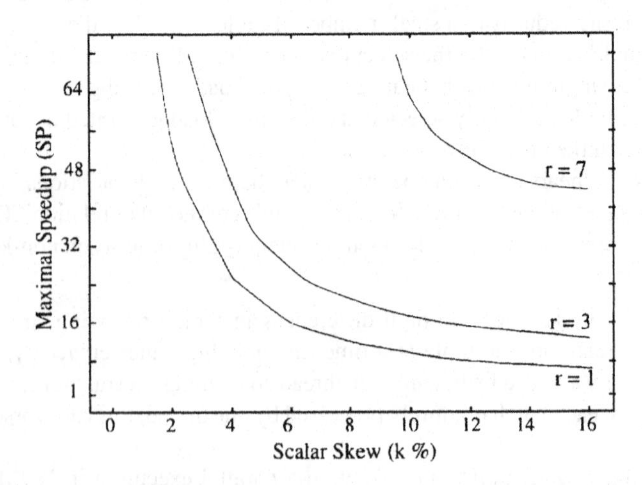


*Figure 4.* Maximal theoretical speed-up.

In NUMA, because the number of processors is higher and the pipeline chains tend to be longer,[4] all these problems are magnified.

## 5. Parallel execution model for NUMA

In this section, we propose a parallel execution model for NUMA which strives to keep the advantages of SP without load unbalancing in case of skew. Since SP does not materialize intermediate tuples, there is no easy way to do load balancing. Our PS strategy is based on partial materialization of intermediate results, using activations [7], in order to enable load redistribution. Load balancing is then achieved by allowing any thread to process any materialized tuple (activation), thus ensuring that no thread will be idle during the query execution.

A naive implementation of this idea could yield high overhead. Public access (by all processors) to intermediate results induces much interference for synchronization. Furthermore, tuple materialization incurs copying and memory consumption. One priority in designing our execution model was to minimize those overheads. Synchronization overhead is reduced by using two execution modes. In *normal mode*, when no processor is idle, partially materialized results can be accessed only by the processors that produced them, thereby avoiding processor interference.[5] In *degraded mode*, i.e., as soon as one processor is idle, intermediate results are progressively made public to allow load redistribution. Furthermore, our implementation avoids data copying and limits memory consumption.

In the rest of this section, we present the basic concepts underlying our model. Then, we present in more details PS in normal and degraded modes. Finally, we illustrate PS with an example.

### 5.1. *Basic concepts*

A simple strategy for obtaining good load balancing is to allocate a number of threads much higher than the number of processors and let the operating system do thread scheduling. However, this strategy incurs a lot of system calls which are due to thread scheduling, interference and convoy problems [4, 21, 37]. Instead of relying on the operating system for load balancing, we choose to allocate only one thread per processor per query. The advantage of this one-thread-per-processor allocation strategy is to significantly reduce the overhead of interference and synchronization.

An *activation* represents the finest unit of sequential work [7]. Two kinds of activations can be distinguished: *trigger activation* used to start the execution of a scan on one page of a relation and *tuple activation* describing a tuple produced in pipeline mode. Since, in our model, any activation may be executed by any thread, activations must be self-contained and reference all information necessary for their execution: the code to execute and the data to process. A trigger activation is represented by an (*Operator, Page*) pair which references the scan operator and the page to scan. A tuple activation is represented by an (*Operator, Tuple, HashTable*) triple which references the operator to process (build or probe), the tuple to process, and the corresponding hash table. For a build operator, the tuple activation specifies that the tuple must be inserted in the hash table. For a probe operator, it specifies that the tuple must be probed with the hash table.

The processing of one activation by one operator implies the creation of one or more activations corresponding to result tuples, for the next operator. These activations are stored in *activation buffers* whose size is a parameter of our model. At any time, a thread has an *input activation buffer* to consume activations and an *output activation buffer* to store result tuples.

Activation buffers associated with an operator are grouped in *activations queues*. To avoid activation copies (from activation buffers to activation queues), only references to buffers are stored in queues. To unify the execution model, queues are used for trigger activations (inputs for scan operators) as well as tuple activations (inputs for build or probe operators). Each operator has a queue to receive input activations, i.e., the pipelined operand. We create one queue per operator and thread. Assuming $p$ processors executing a pipeline chain with $n$ operators numbered from 1 to $n$ (operator $n$ produces the final result), the set of queues can be represented by a matrix $Q$. $Q_{i,j}$ $(i \in [1, n], j \in [1, p])$ represents the queue of thread $j$ associated with operator $i$. A column represents the set of queues associated with a thread while a row represents all the queues associated with an operator. The sizes of the buffers and queues impose a limit to memory consumption during query execution.

Each queue is locked by a semaphore (mutex) to allow concurrent read and write operations. Each thread holds a *queue lock* on all its associated queues at the beginning of the execution. We call *private queue* a queue associated with a thread. During normal execution mode, access to private queues, i.e., *private access*, is restricted to the owner only, thus without synchronization. Degraded execution mode implies releasing some queue locks. When a thread releases a lock on a private queue, the queue becomes *public*. Access to public queues, i.e., *public access*, is allowed to every thread, but with synchronization.

Figure 5 illustrates all these concepts with an initial configuration of our model while executing the last pipeline chain presented in figure 1. There are four operators executed by three threads. Therefore, we have 12 queues, each one protected by a lock. Thread $T_1$ is

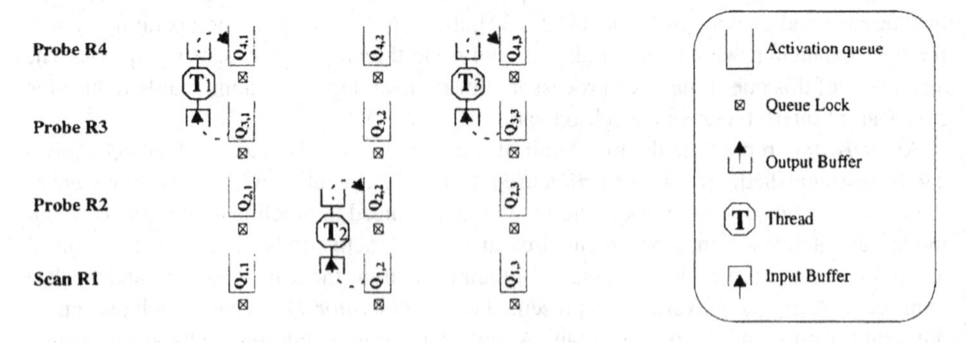


*Figure 5.* Initial configuration of PS.

executing operator *Probe R3*, so its input buffer contains activations from queue $Q_{3,1}$ and writes results in the output buffer, which is flushed in Queue $Q_{4,1}$.

### 5.2. *Execution in normal mode*

During execution in normal mode, a thread consumes and produces activations in its set of private queues (each thread has one private queue for each operator of the pipeline chain), without requiring synchronization.

Processing activations of the pipeline chain proceeds as follows. For each activation (trigger or tuple) of the input buffer, the thread executes the code of the operator referenced by the activation on the corresponding tuples, thus producing activations for the next operator in the output buffer. When an output buffer gets full, its reference is inserted in the queue of the next operator and an empty buffer is allocated. When the input buffer has been entirely processed, it becomes the output buffer of the next operator which becomes current. This process is repeated until the end of the pipeline chain. If the input buffer of the current operator is empty (there are no more activations to process), the thread tries to consume in the queue of the previous operator(s). Thus, when a thread executes an operator, all the queues of the following operators are necessarily empty. In other words, operators at the end of the pipeline chain get consumed in priority with respect to the operators at the beginning. This minimizes the size of intermediate results.

Processing activations of the first operator (scan) is slightly different. At the beginning of execution, trigger activations are inserted in the queues of the scan operator. This is done in a way that maximizes I/O parallelism. For instance, assuming that each processor has its own disk, the trigger activations inserted in $Q_{1,j}$ must yield accesses to disk $j$. Thus, when $p$ threads read in parallel $p$ trigger activations of the scan operator, they also do parallel access to $p$ disks. Trigger activations are processed as follows. The thread first performs a synchronous I/O to read the first page and initiates asynchronous I/Os for the subsequent pages. After reading the first page, the thread selects (and projects) the tuples in the output buffer. When the trigger activation (i.e., one page) has been consumed, the next operator is started and execution proceeds as described above. When the thread comes back to the scan operator (to consume other trigger activations), asynchronous I/Os are likely to be completed and there is no waiting.

A problem occurs when processing an activation produces more tuples than what can be stored in the queue of the next operator. There are two main reasons for this. Either the current activation produces too many results tuples because of data skew, or the memory space allocated to activation buffers and queues is not enough. In either case, the thread suspends its current execution by making a procedure call to process the output activation buffer which cannot be flushed into the full activation queue. Thus, context saving is done efficiently by procedure call, which is much less expensive than operating system-based synchronization (e.g., signals).

To summarize, each activation is processed entirely and its result is materialized. This is different from SP where an activation is always partially consumed. If we consider the tree of tuples produced by a trigger activation (see figure 3), activation consumption is partially breadth-first in PS versus strictly depth-first in SP.

### 5.3. *Execution in degraded mode*

Execution in normal mode continues until one thread gets idle, because there is no more activation to process in any of its private queues. Then, a form of load sharing is needed whereby the other threads make public some of their activations which can then be consumed by the idle thread.

Any thread can make a queue public, simply by releasing the lock it holds since the beginning of execution. After releasing the lock, subsequent access to the queue by all threads (including the initial thread) requires synchronization. To further reduce interference in degraded mode, only a subset of the queues is made public at a time. We use a simple heuristic for the choice and the number of queues to be made public:[6] (i) all queues $Q_{k,j}$ corresponding to operator $k$ are made public together; (ii) operators are chosen in increasing order of the pipeline chain (from 1 to $n$).

At any time, two global indicators are maintained: FirstActiveOp and SharingLevel. *FirstActiveOp* indicates the first active operator in the pipeline chain. Thus, at the beginning of execution, we have $FirstActiveOp = 1$. *SharingLevel* indicates the operator of highest rank whose queues have been made public. At the beginning of execution, we have $SharingLevel = 0$. These two indicators can be updated by any thread and can only increase during execution, i.e., a public queue cannot become private again. Query execution ends when *FirstActiveOp* is $n + 1$.

Query execution can now be summarized as follows. During normal execution, each thread $t$ consumes activations in its private queues $Q_{i,t}$ ($i \in [SharingLevel + 1, n]$), without any synchronization. When it has no more activations in its private queues, a thread attempts to consume activations in the set of public queues ($Q(i, j), i \in [FirstActiveOp, SharingLevel], j \in [1, p]$), by locking them. When no more activations are available in the public queues, *SharingLevel* is increased by 1 which notifies all threads that they must release their lock, i.e., make public the queues associated with operator *SharingLevel*. Notice that a thread may consume activations from public queues during degraded mode but will always produce activations for its private queues.

### 5.4. *Simple example of PS execution*

We now illustrate the main concepts of our model on the example given in figure 1, executing the join of R1, R2, R3 and R4, with three processors and thus three threads. We concentrate on the degraded mode, with one idle thread, which is more interesting. We assume that the join with R2 of tuple t, resulting from the select of R1, produces a high number of tuples for operator *Probe R3* because of product skew. Thread $T_2$ processes this tuple.

Figure 6 gives an execution snapshot when $T_2$ is still producing tuples resulting from joining t with R2. $T_3$ ends processing its activation buffer, coming from queue $Q_{4,3}$. When $T_3$ finishes its last activation, it tries to find new activations in its private queues $Q_{4,3}$ and $Q_{3,3}$. Since it fails, it looks up the public queues $Q_{2,3}$, $Q_{2,2}$ and $Q_{2,1}$, using synchronized accesses. Again, it fails finding activations. So it increments *SharingLevel* and tries to consume in queue $Q_{3,2}$ (which contains activations), however, it gets blocked because $T_2$ is currently holding the lock. When $T_2$ detects the change of *SharingLevel*, it makes public the

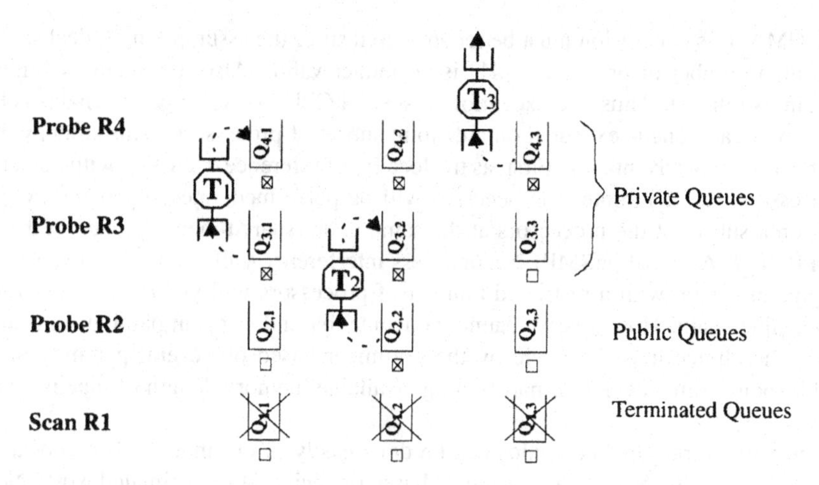


*Figure 6.* A simple example of PS execution.

queue $Q_{3,2}$ by releasing its lock (for further access to this queue, $T_2$ will use synchronized accesses). $T_3$, having requested the lock of $Q_{3,2}$ gets it, and consumes its activations. This produces activations for queue $Q_{4,3}$ (simply because $T_3$ is processing these activations) which can then be stored and consumed by $T_3$ without locking (because it is still private).

Two observations can be made. If *SharingLevel* is rarely tested, $T_3$ can remain blocked on the lock of queue $Q_{3,2}$ for a while. Thus, it is important that *SharingLevel* be often tested. However, since it is potentially accessed by all threads, *SharingLevel* could become a bottleneck. In fact, this does not happen for two reasons. First, each thread frequently accesses *SharingLevel* which gets locally cached. Second, even if writing *SharingLevel* implies invalidating it in each cache, this happens only $n$ times ($n$ is the length of the pipeline chain) which has a negligible effect.[7]

This simple example shows the benefits of using partial materialization of intermediate results, and partial access by all threads to intermediate results.

### 5.5. *Execution of bushy trees*

For simplicity, we have considered the execution of only one pipeline chain. However, our execution model can be easily generalized. We now show how this model can deal with more general bushy trees.

The best parallel plan produced by the optimizer is not necessarily a pure right-deep tree and can well be a bushy tree connecting long pipeline chains. The pros and cons of executing several pipeline chains concurrently in shared-memory are discussed in [21, 41]. The main conclusion is that it would almost never make sense to execute several pipeline chains concurrently since it increases resource consumption (memory and disk). In [41], it is shown that, assuming ideal speed-up, this strategy may be used in only two cases: (i) one pipeline chain is I/O-bound and the other is CPU-bound; (ii) the two pipeline chains access relations which are partitioned over disjoint sets of disks.

In NUMA, this conclusion must be reconsidered since the assumption of ideal speed-up with a high number of processors [41] is no longer valid. Also, the memory limitation constraint is relaxed. Thus, the execution of several CPU-bound[8] pipeline chains is beneficial only if each one is executed on a disjoint subset of processors. This strategy would have the following advantages. First, as the locality of reference decreases with the number of processors, fewer remote data accesses will be performed, specially if the execution occurs on a subset of the processors at the same node (shared-memory node in the Convex'SPP, NUMA-Q and nuSMP). Second, less interference will occur. Finally, executing each pipeline chain with a restricted number of processors will yield better speed-up on each pipeline chain. However, we cannot conclude that independent parallelism is always better. The choice must be made by the optimizer based on several parameters: estimated response time, degree of partitioning, available memory, length of pipeline chains, etc.

Executing several pipeline chains can be done easily in our model. The allocation of pipeline chains to the processors is decided based on their relative estimated work. Normal execution proceeds as before. However, in degraded mode, *SharingLevel* is global to all concurrent pipeline chains. Thus, a public queue can be accessed by any processor, even if it was initially working on a different pipeline chain. This is possible simply because each activation is self-contained. The only necessary modification is to create a number of queues for each thread that is equal to the length of the longest pipeline chain. In this way, load balancing is globally achieved on the set of pipeline chains.

## 6. Performance evaluation

Performance evaluation of a parallel execution model for complex queries is made difficult by the need to experiment with many different queries and large relations. The typical solution is to use simulation which eases the generation of queries and data, and allows testing with various configurations. However, simulation would not allow us to take into account the effect of NUMA as well as important performance aspects such as the overhead of thread interference. On the other hand, using full implementation and benchmarking would restrict the number of queries and make data generation very hard. Therefore, we decided to fully implement our execution model on a NUMA multiprocessor and simulate the execution of operators. To exercise the effect of NUMA, real tuples are actually exchanged, i.e., read and written, but their content is ignored. Thus, query execution does not depend on relation content and can be simply studied by generating queries and setting relation parameters (cardinality, selectivity, skew factor, etc.).

In the rest of this section, we describe our experimentation platform and report on performance results.

### 6.1. *Experimentation platform*

We now introduce the multiprocessor configuration we have used for our experiments and discuss the influence of NUMA on query execution. We also explain how we have

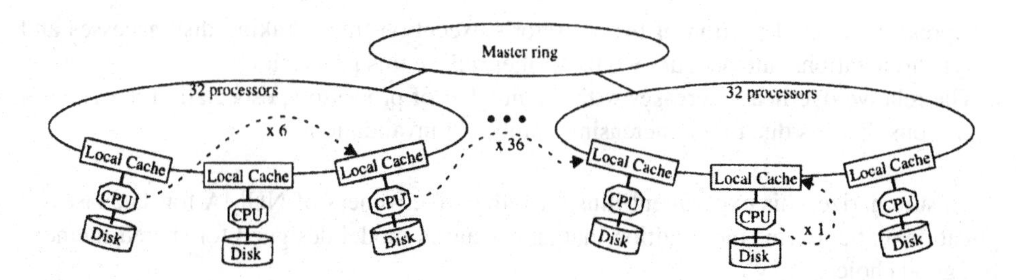


*Figure 7.* KSR1 architecture.

generated parallel execution plans, and present the methodology that was applied in all experiments.

***6.1.1. KSR1 multiprocessor.*** We have implemented SP and PS on a 72-processor KSR1 computer at Inria. Each processor is 40 MIPS and has its own 32 Mbytes memory, called local cache. The KSR1 computer implements the concept of NUMA with a hardware-based shared virtual memory system, called Allcache. The time to access a data item depends on the kind of operation (read, write) and on its location (processor's subcache, local cache, remote cache).

To better understand the effect of virtual shared memory on query execution, we have performed an experiment comparing two basic operators (build and probe) implemented in two different ways: one which exercises NUMA and the other which simulates pure shared-memory. In the NUMA implementation, data accesses are done randomly in any cache (local or remote). In the shared-memory simulation, data accesses are made all local. Each processor accesses 30 MB of data.[9] For the build operator, only references to tuples are written (in the global hash table) whereas, for the probe operator, only a portion (2/3) of the tuple is accessed (to test the matching predicate). In this experiment, there is no I/O and no synchronization. The results are summarized below, as ratios of the NUMA response time versus the simulated shared-memory response time.

| | 16 proc. | 32 proc. | 64 proc. |
|---|---|---|---|
| Build operator | 1.6 | 1.8 | 2.5 |
| Probe operator | 1.2 | 1.3 | 1.6 |

They suggest the following comments:

- Read operations, even intensive, have much less impact on performance than write operations. This is because writing implies broadcasting a cache line invalidation to all processors having a local copy.
- Remote operations have less impact than expected (the KSR technical documentation indicates a factor 6 between local and remote access). This is because memory access

represents a small portion of the operator's execution time. Taking disk accesses and synchronizations into account would further reduce this proportion.
- The relative overhead increases with the number of processors, especially for write operations. This is due to the increasing number of invalidations.

To summarize, this experiment illustrates the effectiveness of NUMA for database application and confirms the intuition that an execution model designed for shared-memory is a good choice.

As only one disk of the KSR1 was available to us, we simulated disk accesses to base relations. One disk per processor was simulated with the following typical parameters:

| Parameter | Value |
|---|---|
| Rotation time [33] | 17 ms |
| Seek time | 5 ms |
| Transfer rate | 6 MB/s |
| Asynchronous I/O init. | 5000 inst. |
| Page size | 8 KB |
| I/O cache size | 8 pages |

***6.1.2. Parallel execution plans.*** The input to our execution model is a parallel execution plan obtained after compilation and optimization of a user query. To generate queries, we use the algorithm given in [41] with three kinds of relations: small (10K–20K tuples), medium (100K–200K tuples) and large (1M–2M tuples). First, an acyclic predicate connection graph for the query is randomly generated. Second, for each relation involved in the query, a cardinality is randomly chosen in one of the small, medium or large ranges. Third, the join selectivity factor of each edge $(R, S)$ in the predicate connection graph is randomly chosen in the range $[0.5 * \min(|R|, |S|)/|R \times S|, 1.5 * \max(|R|, |S|)/|R \times S|]$.

The result of query generation is an acyclic connected graph adorned with relation cardinalities and edge selectivities. We have generated 20 queries, each involving 7 relations. Each query is then run through our DBS3 query optimizer [27] to select the best right-deep tree.

Without any constraint on query generation, we would obtain very different executions which would make it difficult to give meaningful conclusions. Therefore, we constrain the generation of operator trees so that the sequential response time is between 20 and 35 min. Thus, we have produced 20 parallel execution plans involving about 0.7 GB of base relations and about 1.3 GB of intermediate results. Note that executions with too small relations (in particular, internal ones which need to be materialized) would not allow to appreciate the effects of NUMA.

In the following experiments, each point in a graph will be obtained from a computation based on the response times of 20 parallel execution plans. Computing the average response time does not make sense. Therefore, the results will always be in terms of comparable execution times. For instance, in a speed-up experiment, let the speed-up be the ratio of response time with $p$ processors over the response time with one processor, each point will be computed as the average of the speed-ups of all plans. To obtain precise measurements, each response time is computed as the average of five successive measurements.

### 6.2. *Performance comparisons with no skew*

This experiment was done to study the overhead of PS over SP when there is no skew. SP could be easily implemented by changing PS. The only modification we did was to replace the call to the function that store tuples in buffers (and then buffers in queues) by a procedure call to the next operator. Therefore, SP and PS are identical in terms of processing the trigger activations and performing (asynchronous) I/Os. The use of asynchronous I/O instead of multiplexing processors between I/O threads and CPU threads gives a small performance enhancement, because there are less synchronization and fewer system calls.

For PS, the size of the activation buffers is one page (8 KB) and the queue size is fixed to 20 buffer references. Also, a buffer size of 200 KB is allocated per processor. For instance, with 32 processors, a maximum of 6.4 MB of activations can be materialized. These values were experimentally defined and are directly related to the quality of load balancing which can be achieved.

Figure 8(a) shows the average speed-up of all query executions for SP and PS while figure 8(b) the relative performance of PS and SP, i.e., the average of the ratios of PS versus SP response times.[10] We can make two important observations.

First, SP and PS show near-linear speed-up. We may remark that the effects of the nonuniform memory access are also visible with one processor. For instance, with a single processor executing the entire query, the memory of other processors would also be used, because the outer relations do not fit in one processor's local cache. Furthermore, when more processors access the same large amount of data, the overhead implied by NUMA gets parallelized, i.e., the overhead of cache misses are shared between threads. This explains the very good speed-up which we obtain.

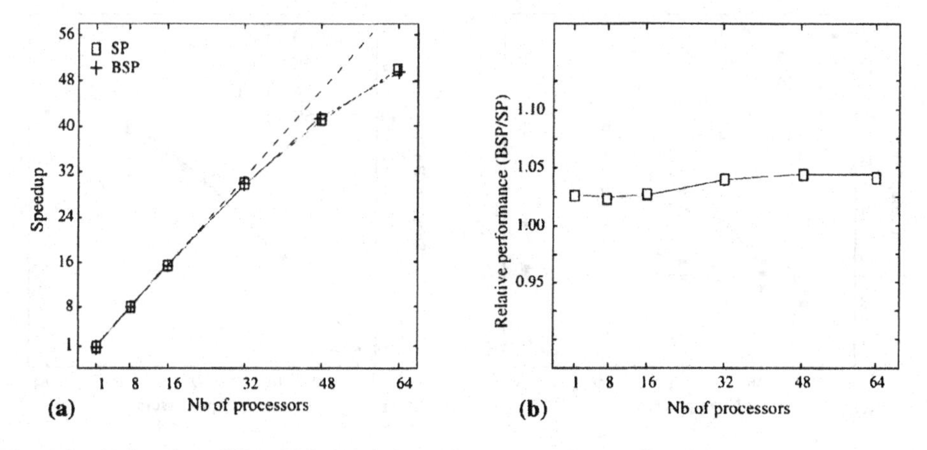


*Figure 8.* (a) Speed-up of SP and PS, (b) relative performance of PS versus SP.

Second, the performance of PS is very close to that of SP (the major difference does not exceed 4%) because the design of PS minimizes the overhead of materializing and sharing tuples. Without skew, execution proceeds in normal mode for almost all processing time (the degraded mode is activated at the end of the execution, but has no significant effect). Thus, there is no synchronization and no interference, even with a high number of threads. Furthermore, SP has no locality of reference [42] because it is always switching from one operator to another. As PS uses buffered input and outputs, it exhibits more locality of reference than SP.

### 6.3. *Impact of data skew*

In this experiment, we study the impact of data skew on the performance of SP and PS. We introduce skew in only one operator, at the $r$th rank of the pipeline chain. One tuple (or one batch for the first operator) of this operator produces $k\%$ of that operator's result. The other operators have no skew, so the production of result tuples is uniform. Such modeling of data skew is called *scalar skew* [13, 36, 48]. We chose to have $k$ between 0 and 6%. This is reasonable and rather optimistic since we consider that only one operator of the pipeline chain has skew.

Figures 9(a) and (b) show the speed-up obtained for SP and PS for different skew factors. The skewed operator is placed at the beginning or in the middle (rank 4) of the pipeline chain. It is obvious that SP suffers much from data skew. With a skew factor of 4% on the first operator, the speed-up is only 22, which means a performance degradation of more than 200% compared with no skew. The theoretical speed-up (as computed in Section 2) is never reached. This is because the skewed tuple can be consumed at any time during the execution. A final remark on SP is that, when the number of processors is less than 10, the effect of skew is much reduced. This confirms the value of SP for small shared-memory multiprocessors.

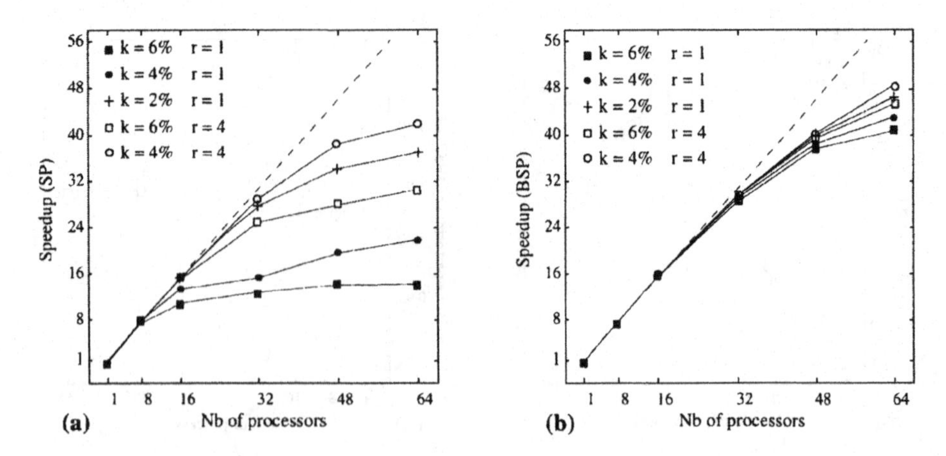


*Figure 9.* (a) Speed-up of SP with skew, (b) speed-up of PS with skew.

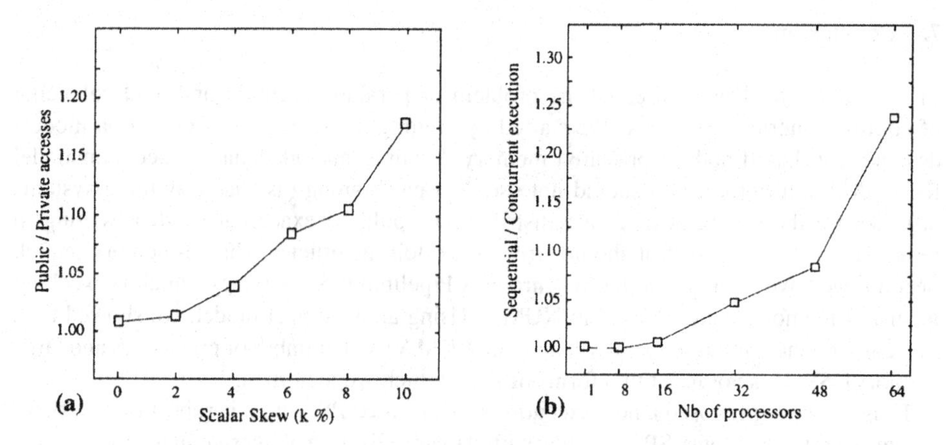


*Figure 10.* (a) Private versus public access, (b) gain of concurrent executions.

The impact of skew on PS is insignificant. Depending on the skew factor, the degraded mode starts sooner or later, producing thread interferences. However, thread interference is minimized by doing progressive load sharing. For instance, when the queues of operators 1 and 2 become public, the other operators (3–7) keep being processed without synchronization. Figure 10(a) shows the variation of the ratio of locked access to queues versus unlocked one with the skew (with 32 processors). We can observe that this ratio stays low (less than 10% with $k = 6\%$) because of our progressive load sharing mechanism.

### 6.4. *Parallel execution of several pipeline chains*

As discussed in Section 4, the concurrent execution of different CPU-bound pipeline chains, each by a disjoint subset of processors, seems better in NUMA because it reduces interference and remote data access, thereby yielding better speed-up.

In this experiment, we use a bushy tree containing three CPU-bound pipeline chains that can be executed concurrently, consisting of 3, 2 and 4 joins. We only consider the execution of these pipeline chains, ignoring the other operators of the bushy tree. We measured the response time of sequential versus concurrent execution of the three pipeline chains. For the concurrent execution, each pipeline chain is executed on a number of processors computed based on a simple estimate of their response time. This is achieved using a very simple cost model to evaluate the complexity of each pipeline chain and making a ratio of the number of processors (as in [22]).

Figure 10(b) shows the gain presented as the ratio of the response time of sequential versus concurrent execution, as a function of the number of processors. With less than three processors, some processors may execute several pipeline chains, thus in a sequential fashion. The gain is steadily increasing and gets significant (24%) with a high number of processors. As the number of processors increases, the speed-up obtained by a sequential execution worsens whereas it gets better for a concurrent execution. This confirms the benefit of executing several pipeline chains concurrently for large NUMA configurations.

## 7. Conclusion

In this paper, we have addressed the problem of parallel execution and load balancing of complex queries in NUMA. We started by arguing the relevance of execution models designed for shared-nothing or shared-memory. We first concluded that an execution model for NUMA multiprocessors should not use data partitioning (as shared-nothing systems do) because the overhead of data redistribution would be exacerbated when writing in remote memories. Instead, it should strive to exploit the efficient shared-memory model. Second, we have argued that the Synchronous Pipelining (SP) strategy which is excellent in shared-memory could be used in NUMA. Using an analytical model, we showed that, as a consequence of the scalability feature of NUMA (high number of processors and large memory), SP does not resist two forms of skew which we identified.

Thus, we have proposed a new execution model called PS, which is robust to data skew. The major difference with SP is to allow partial materialization of intermediate results, made progressively public in order to be processed by any processor which would otherwise be idle. This yields excellent load balancing, even with data skew. In addition, PS can exploit the concurrent execution of several pipeline chains.

To validate PS and study its performance, we have conducted a performance comparison using an implementation of SP and PS on a 72-processor KSR1 (NUMA) computer, with many queries and large relations. With no skew, SP and PS have both near-linear speed-up. However, the impact of skew is very severe on SP performance while it is insignificant on PS. For instance, with a skew factor of 4%, the performance degradation of SP is 200% while it is only 15% with PS. Finally, we have shown that executing several pipeline chains concurrently yields significant performance gains with a high number of processors.

To summarize, the experiments have shown that PS outperforms SP as soon as there is skew and can scale up very well. Although if the measurements have been conducted on the KSR1 (Cache Only Memory Architecture), we can expect the same behavior on Cache Coherent NUMA,[11] ho and pure shared-memory multiprocessors, since no specific feature of the KSR1 was used in our PS strategy. Thus, PS should be considered a strategy of choice for implementing database systems on both shared-memory and NUMA multiprocessors.

## Acknowledgments

The authors wish to thank C. Mohan, B. Dageville and J.R. Gruser for many fruitful discussions on parallel execution models and Jean-Paul Chieze for helping us with the KSR1.

## Notes

1. The goal of our analysis is not to compare different classes of NUMA (see [44, 34] for a discussion), but to propose an effective execution strategy for these architectures.
2. Any algorithm that allows pipeline execution, for example, index join, nested-loop join, pipelined hash join [49] could be used. However, some algorithms can be inefficient in NUMA because of data reorganizations which may incur intensive remote data reading or writing. Studying this issue is beyond the scope of this paper.

3. The performance of the classical partitioned execution model (called Fixed Processing (FP) in [7]) were always worse than DP.
4. Considering a large main memory.
5. Of course, the interferences inherent in SP (I/O, page management, etc.) cannot be avoided.
6. We have tried other appealing heuristics and we obtained similar performance.
7. We use a global variable instead of operating system signals, but the two approaches seem equivalent.
8. The optimization of I/O-bound tasks cannot be done at runtime because it essentially depends on data partitioning on disks.
9. With more than 32 MB of data, a local execution could not be obtained.
10. Speedup measurement is not sufficient since it does not show relative performance.
11. Considering CC-NUMA architecture, however, raises some new issues (e.g., initial configuration).

## References


1. A. Agarwal, R. Bianchini, D. Chaiken, K.L. Johnson, D. Kranz, J. Kubiatowicz, B.-H. Lim, K. Mackenzie, and D. Yeung, "The MIT alewife machine: Architecture and performance," Int. Symp. on Computer Architecture, June 1995.
2. P.M.G. Apers, C.A. van den Berg, J. Flokstra, P.W.P.J. Grefen, M.L. Kersten, and A.N. Wilschut, "PRISMA/DB: A parallel main memory relational DBMS," IEEE Trans. Knowledge and Data Engineering, vol. 4, no. 6, December 1992.
3. A. Bhide, "An analysis of three transaction processing architectures," Int. Conf on VLDB, Los Angeles, August 1988.
4. M. Blasgen, J. Gray, M. Mitoma, and T. Price, "The convoy phenomenon," Operating Systems Review, vol. 13, no. 2, April 1979.
5. H. Boral, W. Alexander, L. Clay, G. Copeland, S. Danforth, M. Franklin, B. Hart, M. Smith, and P. Valduriez, "Prototyping Bubba: A highly parallel database system," IEEE Trans. Knowledge and Data Engineering, vol. 2, no. 1, March 1990.
6. L. Bouganim, B. Dageville, and P. Valduriez, "Adaptative parallel query execution in DBS3," Industrial Paper, Int. Conf. on EDBT Avignon, March 1996.
7. L. Bouganim, D. Florescu, and P. Valduriez, "Dynamic load balancing in hierarchical parallel database systems," Int. Conf. on VLDB, Bombay, September 1996. Can be retrieved at http://rodin.inria.fr/personnes/luc.bouganim/papers/VLDB.html
8. Data General Corporation, "Data general and oracle to optimize oracle universal server for ccNUMA system," can be retrieved at http://www.dg.com/news/press_releases/11_4_96.html
9. Data General Corporation, "The NUMA invasion," can be retrieved at http://www.dg.com/newdocs1/ccnuma/iw1_6_97.html
10. Data General Corporation, "Standard high volume servers: The new building block," can be retrieved at http://www.dg.com/newdocs1/ccnuma/index.html#a
11. D.J. DeWitt, S. Ghandeharizadeh, D. Schneider, A. Bricker, H. Hsiao, and R. Rasmussen, "The gamma database machine project," IEEE Trans. on Knowledge and Data Engineering, vol. 2, no. 1, March 1990.
12. D.J. DeWitt and J. Gray, "Parallel database systems: The future of high performance database processing," Communications of the ACM, vol. 35, no. 6, June 1992.
13. D.J. DeWitt, J.F. Naughton, D.A. Schneider, and S. Seshadri, "Practical skew handling in parallel joins," Int. Conf. on VLDB, Vancouver, August 1992.
14. S. Frank, H. Burkhardt, and J. Rothnie, "The KSR1: Bridging the gap between shared-memory and MPPs," Compcon'93, San Francisco, February 1993.
15. M.N. Garofalakis and Y.E. Yoannidis, "Multi-dimensional resource scheduling for parallel queries," ACM-SIGMOD Int. Conf., Montreal, June 1996.
16. J.R. Goodman and P.J. Woest, "The Wisconsin multicube: A new large-scale cache-coherent multiprocessor," University of Wisconsin-Madison, TR 766, April 1988.
17. G. Graefe, "Volcano: An extensible and parallel dataflow query evaluation system," IEEE Trans. on Knowledge and Data Engineering, vol. 6, no. 1, February 1994.

18. E. Hagersten, E. Landin, and S. Haridi, "Ddm—A cache-only memory architecture," IEEE Computer, vol. 25, no. 9, September 1992.
19. W. Hasan and R. Motwani, "Optimization algorithms for exploiting the parallel communication tradeoff in pipelined parallelism," Int. Conf on VLDB, Santiago, 1994.
20. Y. Hirano, T. Satoh, A.U. Inoue, and K. Teranaka, "Load balancing algorithms for parallel database processing on shared memory multiprocessors," Int. Conf. on Parallel and Distributed Information Systems, Miami Beach, December 1991.
21. W. Hong, "Exploiting inter-operation parallelism in XPRS," ACM-SIGMOD Int. Conf., San Diego, June 1992.
22. H. Hsiao, M.S. Chen, and P.S. Yu, "On parallel execution of multiple pipelined hash joins," ACM-SIGMOD Int. Conf., Minneapolis, May 1994.
23. IEEE Computer Society, "IEEE standard for scalable coherent interface (SCI)," IEEE Std 1596, New York, August 1992.
24. Intel Corporation, "Standard high volume servers: Changing the rules for buiseness computing," can be retrieved at http://www.intel.com/procs/servers/feature/shv/
25. M. Kitsuregawa and Y. Ogawa, "Bucket spreading parallel hash: A new, robust, parallel hash join method for data skew in the super database computer," Int. Conf on VLDB, Brisbane, 1990.
26. J. Kuskin, D. Ofelt, M. Heinrich, J. Heinlein, R. Simoni, K. Gharachorloo, J. Chapin, D. Nakahira, J. Baxter, M. Horowitz, A. Gupta, M. Rosenblum, and J. Hennessy, "The Stanford FLASH multiprocessor," Int. Symp. on Computer Architecture, April 1994.
27. R. Lanzelotte, P. Valduriez, and M. Zait, "On the effectiveness of optimization search strategies for parallel execution spaces," Int. Conf. on VLDB, Dublin, August 1993.
28. D. Lenoski, J. Laudon, K. Gharachorloo, W.D. Weber, A. Gupta, J. Henessy, M. Horowitz, and M.S. Lam, "The Stanford dash multiprocessor," IEEE Computer, vol. 25, no. 3, March 1992.
29. D. Lenoski, J. Laudon, T. Joe, D. Nakahira, L. Stevens, A. Gupta, and J. Hennessy, "The DASH prototype: Logic overhead and performance," IEEE Transactions of Parallel and Distributed Systems, vol. 4, no. 1, January 1993.
30. M.L. Lo, M-S. Chen, C.V. Ravishankar, and P.S. Yu, "On optimal processor allocation to support pipelined hash joins," ACM-SIGMOD Int. Conf., Washington, May 1993.
31. T. Lovett and R. Clapp, "STiNG: A CC-NUMA computer system for the commercial marketplace," Int. Symp. on Computer Architecture, May 1996.
32. H. Lu, M.-C. Shan, and K.-L. Tan, "Optimization of multi-way join queries for parallel execution," Int. Conf. on VLDB, Barcelona, September 1991.
33. M. Metha and D. DeWitt, "Managing intra-operator parallelism in parallel database systems," Int. Conf. on VLDB, Zurich, September 1995.
34. C. Morin, A. Gefflaut, M. Banâtre, and A.M. Kermarrec, "COMA: An opportunity for building fault-tolerant scalable shared memory multiprocessors," Int. Symp. on Computer Architectures, 1996.
35. M.C. Murphy and M.-C. Shan, "Execution plan balancing," IEEE Int. Conf. on Data Engineering, Kobe, April 1991.
36. E. Omiecinski, "Performance analysis of a load balancing hash-join algorithm for a shared-memory multiprocessor," Int. Conf on VLDB, Barcelona, September 1991.
37. H. Pirahesh, C. Mohan, J. Cheng, T.S. Liu, and P. Selinger, "Parallelism in relational database systems: Architectural issues and design approaches," Int. Symp. on Databases in Parallel and Distributed Systems, Dublin, July 1990.
38. E. Rahm and R. Marek, "Dynamic multi-resource load balancing in parallel database systems," Int. Conf. on VLDB, Zurich, Switzerland, September 1993.
39. D. Schneider and D. DeWitt, "A performance evaluation of four parallel join algorithms in a shared-nothing multiprocessor environment," ACM-SIGMOD Int. Conf., Portland, May-June 1989.
40. A. Shatdal and J.F. Naughton, "Using shared virtual memory for parallel join processing," ACM-SIGMOD Int. Conf., Washington, May 1993.
41. E.J. Shekita and H.C. Young, "Multi-join optimization for symmetric multiprocessor," Int. Conf. on VLDB, Dublin, August 1993.
42. A.J. Smith, "Cache memories," ACM Computing Surveys, vol. 14, no. 3, September 1982.

43. J. Srivastava and G. Elsesser, "Optimizing multi-join queries in parallel relational databases," Int. Conf. on Parallel and Distributed Information Systems, San Diego, January 1993.
44. P. Stenstrom, T. Joe, and A. Gupta, "Comparative performance evaluation of cache-coherent NUMA and COMA architectures," Int. Symp. on Computer Architecture, May 1992.
45. P. Valduriez, "Parallel database systems: Open problems and new issues," Int. Journal on Distributed and Parallel Databases, vol. 1, no. 2, 1993.
46. P. Valduriez and G. Gardarin, "Join and semi-join algorithms for a multiprocessor database machine," ACM Trans. on Database Systems, vol. 9, no. 1, March 1984.
47. C.A. van den Berg and M.L. Kersten, "Analysis of a dynamic query optimization technique for multi-join queries," Int. Conf. on Information and Knowledge Engineering, Washington, 1992.
48. C.B. Walton, A.G. Dale, and R.M. Jenevin, "A taxonomy and performance model of data skew effects in parallel joins," Int. Conf. on VLDB, Barcelona, September 1991.
49. A.N. Wilshut, J. Flokstra, and P.G. Apers, "Parallel evaluation of multi-join queries," ACM-SIGMOD Int. Conf., San Jose, 1995.